Self-Care Activities *for* Women

101 Practical Ways to *Slow Down* and *Reconnect* With Yourself

Cicely Horsham-Brathwaite, PhD

callisto publishing
an imprint of Sourcebooks

*To my foremothers whose love,
faith, perseverance, and sacrifices
seeded the ground for me to thrive.
I thank and honor you.*

Contents

Introduction

Across cultures, there are common themes associated with gender. Women are often socialized to prioritize the needs of others and see their own needs as secondary or even selfish. They often feel that they have no choice but to take care of others first, which leaves them short on time, resources, and energy to take care of themselves. This leads to stress, burnout, and lower life satisfaction.

For these reasons, and many others, it is important to explore the question: What does it mean to take care of yourself? *Self-care* can be defined as "the actions one takes on their own behalf in service of their well-being." Although there is a growing body of research that supports the notion that self-care is important, even necessary, for women's health and well-being, societal (and familial and internal) messaging that self-care is "selfish" persists. These messages are untrue and unhelpful, and I hope that by practicing the activities in this book, you will experience more joy and fulfillment.

I have helped a wide range of women prioritize self-care through my coaching and therapy practice over the last two decades. You will notice how much more able you are to show up for the people in your life and take care of your responsibilities when you have cared for yourself. I hope you'll notice that self-care, as mental health advocate Katie Reed says, "means giving the world the best of you instead of what is left of you."

Some of the biggest barriers to getting started are knowing where to start and how. By picking up this book, you've taken a first, essential step to engaging in more self-care. I'm honored to help guide you on your journey. The chapters of this book are organized by the key types of self-care—emotional, physical, mental, social, and professional—in order to support you in tending to your whole self.

EMOTIONAL SELF-CARE

Adults tend to believe that their actions are based on carefully thought-out plans and rational decisions. The truth is that emotions often drive decisions and behaviors, and you can exert more thoughtful control when you support your emotions through self-care. Emotional self-care means paying attention to your emotions and seeing them as a signal that you have an underlying need that requires a response. When you practice emotional self-care, you honor your emotions with compassion, sit with them, and release them when necessary. The activities in this chapter promote self-care by taking the time and space to notice, engage, and support your emotions.

PHYSICAL SELF-CARE

Your body is a wondrous machine that supports you in a myriad of ways. It also requires conscious effort to give it the attention that it needs to continue to work optimally. Societal messages about women's bodies can lead many to become hyperfocused on how their bodies look rather than on how they *feel*. The activities in this chapter will help you practice physical self-care by engaging in healthy habits and finding strength, pride, and joy in your body and by mitigating the physical impacts of stress.

MENTAL SELF-CARE

Each day, with or without your awareness, you take in numerous messages about how you should look, feel, and act; about what you should like, dislike, focus on; and about what you should prioritize, ignore, and fear. These messages are an unavoidable part of the ecosystem (e.g., schools, media, social, and cultural institutions), and they heavily influence women's identity development and thought patterns. Sadly, many of the messages erode mental health and well-being. The activities in this chapter will help you practice mental self-care to combat the influence of these relentless messages. You can practice mental self-care by becoming aware of your thoughts and shifting those that are unhelpful. Caring for your mental health will allow you to reflect on thought patterns and self-talk, learn ways to soothe, engage, and grow your mind, and counteract societal messages to create your own affirming messages. Thoughts and emotions are intimately related to each other—what you think affects your emotions, and what you feel influences your thoughts. Therefore, you will notice some overlap between the emotional and mental self-care chapters.

SOCIAL SELF-CARE

Self-care is a bit of a misnomer in this context. Although the term does direct you to engage in activities to support your personal well-being, it does not mean merely to focus on self-care in isolation. Communal self-care has helped cultural groups survive and thrive across centuries. Taking care of yourself in community with others provides social support, which is a key factor for coping with physical and mental health challenges and can serve as a preventive measure for developing or exacerbating illness. The activities in this chapter will help you build and maintain nourishing social connections and find joy in the company of others.

PROFESSIONAL SELF-CARE

On average, people spend more time during waking hours in pursuit of professional endeavors than on any other activity. Research indicates that work environments and work responsibilities have a direct effect on your mental health and well-being and present opportunities for joy and challenge. Professional self-care is about consciously creating a professional life that is satisfying and allows you to feel well and thrive. Self-care in this domain refers to the actions you take while working to feel positive, actions you take to craft a meaningful career, and things you can do to create harmony between your work and personal life. The activities in this chapter help you practice self-care by finding balance and meaning in your relationship to work—be it in an office, the home, or anywhere in between.

How to Use This Book

This book provides a step-by-step guide to cultivating more self-care and joy in your life. Each of the 101 activities provides the scientific or conceptual perspectives that support it as well as a supplies list and the time needed. If you experience guilt or discomfort while completing these activities, please know that it could be because our culture does not prioritize emotional, energetic, and physical needs. It may feel challenging to go against the grain and focus on your needs, but change often involves some discomfort as your brain gets used to new patterns. These emotions aren't a sign that you are doing something wrong. In fact, they will likely show up as you learn new habits that promote your well-being.

Whenever you open the book, take a moment to connect with yourself and reflect upon what type of self-care you need, whether it be physical or emotional or something else. I recommend trying each activity that fits your context at least once. After doing so, create a short list of five to six activities from each chapter to try two more times, and notice which ones bring about the most relief or joy. These can become your go-to self-care activities. You might benefit from having the same daily practice, or you might prefer to be intuitively guided by your mood and body each day. The important thing is to prioritize self-care and make it a part of your regular routine. Feel free to use the space in the back of the book to capture any thoughts or feelings that arise while developing your self-care.

Please note that the activities in this book are meant for educational purposes only and are not a substitute for medical or mental health care. Please seek support from a licensed professional if you are experiencing any symptoms or distress.

CHAPTER 1

Emotional Self-Care

Create Your Joy Playlist

ACTIVITY TIME:
1 hour

SUPPLIES:
Device with internet access

Headphones or speakers

When you engage in certain activities, your brain releases neurotransmitters (chemical messengers that send signals from one neuron to another) that affect your emotional state and perceptions. Dopamine is a neurotransmitter that helps stimulate the reward centers in your brain. Listening to pleasurable music is a dopamine trigger; it can create a feeling of happiness in your body. In this activity, harness the power of dopamine by curating a playlist of upbeat songs that lift or shift your mood. Listen the first time without distractions so you notice how your mood shifts.

1. Create a list of songs that bring about positive memories or feelings.

2. Review your songs one by one and notice what emotions emerge.

3. Cross off any songs on the list that are attached to negative feelings until you have a playlist of ten songs that brings about the most positive feelings.

4. Name your playlist something special that brings a smile to your face.

5. Make time in your calendar that matches the total listening time of your playlist.

6. Take note of your mood just before starting.

7. At the appointed time, play your songs, and do not multitask. Feel free to dance!

8. Take note of your mood when the last song plays.

9. Play it whenever you need a mood shift.

Release Your Distractions

ACTIVITY TIME:
30 minutes

SUPPLIES:
Journal or paper

Pen

Most people have a set of go-to activities to help them cope with emotions that come from dealing with daily stressors. This can be binge-watching their favorite shows or scrolling social media sites. Though the goal is to find relief, when distraction is the only coping strategy, you cannot address the underlying issues. Other alternative self-care actions, such as tuning in, noticing what you need, and giving yourself that very thing will bring true relief, not just distraction. It might be a bath, walk, reading, having tea, meditating, or exercising.

1. Write a list of your potential pseudo-regulators and when you engage in them.

2. Take a slow breath in and a slow breath out.

3. Say silently to yourself (or aloud), "I'm going to review my list with curiosity and self-compassion."

4. Review the items on the list, and pick one that you would like to try replacing with alternate activities.

5. Brainstorm a list of alternative activities you can do instead of the pseudo-regulator.

6. Pick one activity and engage in it for fifteen minutes daily over the next week, just before moving to your pseudo-regulator.

7. At the end of the week, see if you would like to switch to the new soothing activity and release the pseudo-regulator.

Name That Emotion

ACTIVITY TIME:

5 minutes

SUPPLIES:

Device with internet
access

Being able to notice and label emotions can help you make better decisions and figure out how to soothe yourself. Identifying your emotion allows you to move from the emotional center of your brain to the planning and processing centers while also lessening the intensity of the emotion. Here you'll practice bringing attention to your emotions, labeling them, and noticing how you feel afterward. By doing so, you take the opportunity to nurture yourself, strengthen your emotional coping skills, and increase your confidence in expressing your emotions to trusted people in your life. In turn, this can deepen your relationships and connection with others.

1. Look up a graphic of human emotion, such as the Gottman Institute's Feeling Wheel.

2. Identify a recent situation where you felt a light or moderate positive emotion. On a scale of 0 (low) to 10 (high), aim for a situation that registered in the 2-to-5 range.

3. List three words from the emotion wheel that match your emotions from that situation.

4. Next, identify a recent situation where you felt a light or moderate negative emotion. Look at your emotion wheel and list three words describing your emotions in that situation.

5. Keep this list and the wheel handy so you can practice naming your emotions in other situations.

6. Over time, practice naming other emotions to expand your list.

Savor the Positive

ACTIVITY TIME:
5 minutes

SUPPLIES:
Timer

Positive emotions are a core component of well-being, but your brain is hardwired to identify and respond to perceived threats in the environment. From a biological perspective, this makes sense, but it also trains the brain to spot and hold on to negative emotions over positive ones. Retrain your brain by noticing and savoring positive emotions. Start with this activity where you will recall a person, pet, or place that you associate with positive emotions, and practice self-care by luxuriating for a few minutes in the feeling that the image brings up.

1. Find a quiet place where you won't be disturbed for at least five minutes.

2. Sit in a comfortable position.

3. Set your timer for five minutes.

4. Identify a person, pet, or place that brings about positive emotions.

5. Recall a specific positive memory related to what you've identified.

6. Close your eyes and breathe in and out at your own pace.

7. Focus on the image in your mind's eye until your timer goes off.

8. When the timer chimes, open your eyes, and turn it off.

9. Take three deep breaths and notice your positive emotional state.

Shake It Off!

ACTIVITY TIME:
5 minutes

SUPPLIES:
None

During the day, you likely face multiple stressors that you cope with but don't have a chance to release. Instead of powering through your day, it's helpful to find or create moments of emotional recovery rather than holding on to the impact of the stress that you face. When you don't mitigate the impact of daily stress, it piles up and can lead to you feeling overwhelmed, burned-out, and even physically ill. For this activity, address stress by shaking, allowing it to move through your body. Shaking engages your parasympathetic nervous system and sends messages that calm your body.

1. Stand or sit as you are able.

2. Rate your level of stress on a scale from 0 (low) to 10 (high).

3. Raise your forearms toward the center of your body and place your hands roughly in front of your heart. You can choose another body part to shake if this motion is not available to you.

4. Shake your hands up and down with your arms flapping ten times.

5. Release your arms alongside your body.

6. Repeat this shaking motion with each leg as you are able.

7. Notice how your body feels, and decide whether to repeat the activity.

8. Rate your level of stress again on a scale from 0 (low) to 10 (high).

Embrace the In-Between

ACTIVITY TIME:
20 minutes

SUPPLIES:
Paper
Pen or Pencil

Life transitions can bring about an intense range of emotions. Change can be uncomfortable. It's important to realize that discomfort is not bad; it is simply a signal that there is more to uncover. That period of discomfort, or the gap between what your life looks like now and what it will look like when the period of transition is over, is liminal space. Allow yourself to trust that you have the resources to navigate the in-between. For this activity, select an in-between in your life right now—it might be watching your kids go to school for the first time, leaving for college, or switching careers—and practice moving through it.

1. On one piece of paper, write today's date. On a second, write the date you anticipate completing the transition. On a third, write a date halfway between the start and expected end dates.

2. Lay each sheet of paper on the floor in chronological order, about a foot apart.

3. Stand before the first sheet of paper and allow yourself to feel the emotions around being where you are right now.

4. Move to the second piece of paper. Imagine being at the halfway point when you've made some progress toward your desired outcome; notice the thoughts and feelings that come up.

5. At the third sheet, consider the emotions and thoughts that arise, imagining you're on the other side of that transition.

6. Spend a few moments journaling about any insights on how you are coping with the transition.

Get Grounded!

ACTIVITY TIME:
3 minutes

SUPPLIES:
Your imagination

Moving through modern life can be hectic and leave people feeling like they're always "on." Frankly, having all the modern conveniences at your fingertips can complicate your life and make it challenging to tune into your bodily rhythms. Luckily, nature provides abundant resources to help you slow down and pay attention to natural rhythms. Doing so can bring about a sense of calm and lift your mood. Here, you'll harness the power of nature and envision grounding to the earth to allow yourself to feel balanced and solid no matter where you are.

1. Sit on the ground or in a chair, based on your comfort and ability.

2. Close your eyes and adjust your body until you feel comfortable.

3. Imagine a palm tree in front of you within arm's reach.

4. Imagine wrapping your hands around the tree and feeling its strength and connection to the earth.

5. Imagine in your mind's eye that the palm tree moves from side to side gently in the wind, knowing that its connection to the earth allows it to move in the flow.

6. Imagine yourself being rooted to the earth and all the resources it provides, just like the palm tree.

7. Continue here until you are ready to stop and return to your day.

8. As you move through the rest of your day, approach situations with the grounded energy you took from this exercise.

Celebrate Yourself!

ACTIVITY TIME:
30 minutes

SUPPLIES:
Music
Snacks
Journal or phone

You don't need a special occasion to celebrate yourself and revel in your uniqueness. You can do it any day, at any time. Acknowledging yourself provides a sense of achievement and positive emotions, which are core components of well-being. Self-acknowledgment is one component of addressing imposter syndrome (i.e., the belief that you are a fraud despite evidence to the contrary) and can help you see yourself more accurately. To prepare for this activity, schedule a celebration date with your-self by placing it in your calendar and telling your loved ones you are only available in case of emergencies.

1. Pick a location where you can spend time alone and celebrate without interruption.

2. At the allotted time, dress in something that makes you feel special. Consider putting on jewelry, makeup, or your favorite shirt, like you are going out to celebrate someone else.

3. Play music that you enjoy. You might even use your joy playlist (Create Your Joy Playlist, page 2).

4. Have your favorite beverages or snacks, if you'd like, and eat them slowly to enjoy the flavor.

5. Record in a notebook, your notes app, or an audio app on your phone all the ways that you are brilliant, unique, gorgeous, kind, and otherwise phenomenal.

6. Revel in your amazingness for at least thirty minutes or until you're ready to stop.

Self-Judgment Time-Out

ACTIVITY TIME:
15 minutes

SUPPLIES:
None

An often underrated but hugely important aspect of life is having rest and downtime. Rest may feel antithetical to reaching goals, but, in fact, it is necessary to take a rest and recharge to achieve them. It does require planning and follow-through. Emotional rest is about taking a break from emotions that weigh you down, self-recrimination, stress, feelings of inferiority, criticism, comparing yourself to others, or thinking about what you haven't accomplished for the day. You will likely find that taking this form of rest brings relief and a sense of lightness.

1. Say "yes" out loud and notice the sensations in your body.

2. Say "no" and notice the sensations in your body.

3. Ask yourself, "Is it okay to give myself a fifteen-minute break from judgment?"

4. When you receive a "yes," move to step 5.

5. For fifteen minutes, engage in an activity purely for enjoyment but without screens. Consider dancing, reading a book, meditating, taking a walk, or just sitting in silence.

6. During this time, notice if any judgment or negative emotions arise in your body. If so, gently say to yourself, "I'm choosing a break from judgment. I am choosing self-compassion," and return to your joyful activity until the time is up.

Childhood Brilliance

ACTIVITY TIME:
10 minutes

SUPPLIES:
None

Social scientists have long debated the impact of genetics versus environment and which is more dominant in shaping individuals. Either way, the environment and culture within which you were raised did contribute to your developing self. Culture and environment often teach girls that they should be humble, acceptable, and appealing to the world. Those social norms do not, however, account for your unique identity, interest, or beliefs, so they may leave you with feelings of self-doubt. There was a time before you were consciously aware of how a girl "should" be where you likely felt fierce and in your full power. For this activity, return to that early version of yourself.

1. Think back to a time in your earlier life before age eight when you felt powerful, and picture what you looked like then.

2. In your mind's eye, invite the little girl version of you to talk with you and share what makes her feel powerful.

3. Thank her for sharing her experience with you, and ask her if you can take some of these lessons back to your everyday life.

4. The next time you are in a situation where you begin to doubt yourself and your power, recall the lessons and emotions you felt when your younger self shared her brilliance.

5. Use that information to help you navigate self-doubt.

Spark Your Creativity!

ACTIVITY TIME:
5 minutes

SUPPLIES:
Smartphone or notepad

You have a creative way of seeing the world that is as unique as you are, a way that you may have taken for granted when you were a child. There are many emotional health and well-being benefits of creativity in adulthood, including stress reduction and engendering a sense of joy. Children have opportunities for creative expression in art classes and imaginary play. Creative moments in adulthood can be less obvious, but paying attention to creative sparks throughout your day and chronicling them will increase your awareness of the wonder within you. In this activity, you'll experience the joy of creating novel solutions in the real world.

1. On your phone or notepad, create a new note with the headline "My Creative Sparks."

2. As you go through your day, pay attention to how you solve life's everyday situations and problems.

3. Record any circumstance in your day-to-day life that requires a creative solution in your "My Creative Sparks" note.

4. Take note of the creative solutions that you used or creative ideas that emerged.

5. Write a sentence or two about the outcome and how you feel about yourself because you used your creativity.

Art Gazing

ACTIVITY TIME:

10 minutes

SUPPLIES:

Three museum art books
  or printed images

Timer

There is evidence from neuroscience research that staring at a work of art has a calming impact on the body and a positive effect on the brain by (1) reducing the stress hormone cortisol; and (2) increasing serotonin and endorphins, neurotransmitters responsible for happiness. Although seeing artwork in a museum or gallery is one option, gazing at works of art from the comfort of your home can also bring the same benefits and allow you to access them whenever you desire. For this activity, look at art daily to lift your mood at the start of your day.

1. Think of an artist you like or do an internet search to find art you enjoy.

2. Acquire a physical copy of this art, whether that's a book or simply printouts that you can interact with without using a screen.

3. After breakfast every morning, pick one of your images.

4. Set a timer for ten minutes.

5. Sit down in a quiet room and look at the picture you chose for the duration of your ten-minute period.

6. Once the alarm rings, turn it off, and decide if you want to sit and stare longer.

7. Whenever you feel you are finished, take note of how you feel, and go on with your day.

Wind Down with Gratitude

ACTIVITY TIME:
15 minutes

SUPPLIES:
Phone

Being aware of gratitude makes people see the world in a better light and makes them happier, even during times filled with stress and trauma. Gratitude strengthens resilience and overall well-being and has been shown to reduce stress, anxiety, and depression. Sharing and receiving gratitude amplifies its effects, because you get to savor your gratitude and that of your companion. This activity builds on research findings that suggest debriefing with someone daily can buffer against burnout.

1. Set up a time when you and a close friend can talk for ten minutes at the end of each day.

2. Whenever something happens during the day that gives you delight or provides you with a sense of appreciation, record a message on your phone. Create a voice memo using dictation software. Alternatively, you can write down these moments in a place that is easy to share, like a note, document, or email.

3. At the end of the day, listen to what you have recorded, and relive those moments.

4. Contact your trusted friend and exchange your day's entries. Listen to their moments.

5. Process the emotions that came from experiencing the day's events with your friend.

6. Try this for one week and continue after that if you find it enjoyable and helpful.

Affirm Your Life

ACTIVITY TIME:
10 minutes

SUPPLIES:
Sticky note

Pen

People use affirmations to create a mindset or reality that doesn't currently exist in their lives. You can also use affirmations to sustain and enhance what is already happening in your life. Doing so helps deepen your awareness of yourself and allows you to celebrate yourself and seek new opportunities to create more abundance in the qualities you affirm. When you use affirmations over time, they can create positive shifts in your self-identity and change negative thought patterns into positive ones that yield positive emotions.

1. Think about the past year, and ask yourself about the events that brought you the most joy.

2. Notice any patterns in the types of circumstances that bring you joy by asking yourself questions like: Who was I with? What did we do? What was unique about the event or experience?

3. With those joyful events in mind, translate them into an affirmation, such as "I surround myself with positive people who laugh, have fun, and are willing to try new things" or "I spend quiet time with myself to recharge and reset to center my joy."

4. Post your affirmation somewhere you can see it, and repeat it at least once a day.

Create a Meaningful Feelings Acronym

ACTIVITY TIME:
20 minutes

SUPPLIES:
Paper

Pen

Acronyms are helpful memory tools and can be used to create reminders that are unique to you. You can craft an acronym that stands for the desired feelings you want to focus on in your everyday life, place it in a prominent location in your home, and/or repeat it to yourself when you need. For example, you could use the acronym JOY if you'd like to focus on being jovial, optimistic, and youthful. Using your acronym like a mantra can help you reset your mindset toward positive emotions.

1. Take an inventory of the feelings you have had over the past seven days, both positive and negative. Refer to the emotion wheel cited in the Name That Emotion (page 5) activity if you need inspiration.

2. Write down the emotions that you have noticed surface often.

3. Of those, circle the top ones that dominated your days.

4. If you circled negative emotions, write down the opposites of them.

5. Create an acronym from these positive emotions, such as HOP for Hopeful, Optimistic, and Proud.

6. Repeat the acronym to yourself throughout your day to charge it with positive emotion.

Emotional Expenditures

ACTIVITY TIME:
20 minutes

SUPPLIES:
Calendar

Taking stock of your emotional output can do much the same thing as budgeting your finances: It provides guidance on how you will want to manage your emotional energy going forward. As you go through your week, you might be unaware of the impact of daily events on your mood and emotions. When you pay attention to the emotions that daily events engender, however, you can determine what to do to amplify positive emotions or render negative emotional expenditures more neutral. This can entail taking negative emotional outputs off your calendar and filling it with more positive events.

1. Look at last month's calendar.

2. Color-code items that were mostly positive in green and events that were mostly negative in red; leave them unshaded if they were neutral events without a strong emotional direction.

3. Review the calendar, and note any trends you see across the colors in the events and what that means for your energy budgeting week by week.

4. Consider whether you can approach any of the neutral or negative events differently to yield positive emotions in the future—for example, by practicing a self-care activity beforehand to tend to your mood before the event.

5. If nothing comes to mind, consider whether you can remove any negative events to yield an overall more positive emotional experience the following week.

Feed Your Soul

ACTIVITY TIME:
Variable

SUPPLIES:
Groceries

Cooking utensils

Smartphone or other recording device

Everyone has culture—familial, ethnic, national, regional—and one of the ways people demonstrate theirs is through food. The preparation methods and seasoning people use are deeply cultural. Often food that nurtures the soul has a connection to childhood and adolescence. I find that one way to care for myself emotionally, tap into feelings of love and nurturing, and ground myself is to reacquaint myself with foods from my family's culture. These foods take me back to a time when I was younger and felt love and compassion from my elders. I do this through cooking lessons from elders in my family, going to restaurants associated with my culture, and trying new recipes.

1. Ask a family member (someone who maintains family recipes or culture) to teach you a family recipe that holds special meaning for you.

2. Go grocery shopping.

3. Set up the workspace for cooking.

4. Set up the device to record the cooking session and hit record.

5. Work alongside your family member, following their instructions as you prepare the meal.

6. While cooking, ask them to share memories that include the dish you are making.

7. Enjoy the meal by mindfully savoring the smell, texture, and taste.

Texting to Catch Up

ACTIVITY TIME:
10 minutes

SUPPLIES:
Smartphone

There are a lot of numbers in your phone book, and likely only a few you call or text regularly. Now is the time to catch up with someone. Sending a positive message to a friend or acquaintance you've lost touch with will likely bring a smile to both your faces. Connecting with others in this way provides an opportunity to recall the good times you have shared, and it's likely to bring about positive emotions that support you in the present. Contact someone who you were on good terms with and who will welcome your outreach, and don't do it for the response. Rather, do it for the emotional boost of reaching out to someone who made you feel happy in the past.

1. Open up your contact list.

2. Find a friend from the past who you have not talked to in a while and would like to reconnect with because you lost touch on good terms.

3. Write your version of the following type of message: "HEY THERE: haven't chatted in a while and was just thinking about you . . . have a great day."

4. Savor the positive emotions that come from that brief connection. If they respond and continue the conversation, consider it a bonus.

Color Your Day!

ACTIVITY TIME:
18 minutes

SUPPLIES:
Paper

Pens, crayons,
   or colored pencils

Coloring and doodling can have many emotional benefits, such as helping to calm your mind and relax. When you focus and immerse yourself in a creative activity, it can help clear your mind of challenging thoughts, which in turn can help relax your body and soothe emotions. In this activity, you will express yourself freely through coloring. Yes, like you did when you were a child! Although this activity supports your emotional well-being, it is also an opportunity to bring more fun into your life.

1. Pick one day in your week when you can spend fifteen minutes coloring or doodling, and mark it on your calendar.

2. At the appointed time, take out your items, and create whatever image comes to mind.

3. Try to use a variety of colors and draw different shapes and elements.

4. Allow your creativity to emerge without judging your results.

5. After you are done, notice how you feel.

6. Take two minutes to savor the image you have created.

7. Congratulate yourself on taking the time for yourself.

Give Yourself a Hug

ACTIVITY TIME:
1 minute

SUPPLIES:
Timer

Giving and receiving hugs has many important benefits for your body, mind, and spirit. Hugs can reduce inflammation, lower stress hormones, strengthen immunity, and trigger the release of oxytocin, sometimes referred to as "the love hormone" because it enables people to bond with and be there to support others. It turns out that many of the same benefits that exist when you hug others also exist when you hug yourself. You can soothe and deepen your relationship with yourself with something as simple as giving yourself a hug. How cool is that?

1. Take your dominant hand and place it on the upper part of your arm, about midway between your elbow and shoulder.

2. Take the opposite hand and place it in the same position between the elbow and shoulder.

3. Lightly squeeze your arms with your hands.

4. With your hands still in place, breathe in and out at your own pace.

5. Close your eyes, and gently rock from side to side.

6. Continue hugging and rocking for a minimum of forty-five seconds.

7. Open your eyes, release your hands, and bring your arms back to your lap.

A Good Cry

ACTIVITY TIME:
2 hours

SUPPLIES:
Device to watch a movie

By necessity, infants cry to communicate their needs and emotional state. As children grow, they receive messages about when it's acceptable to cry and when it is not. As people age, they can have difficulty crying to relieve stress or emotions, even when they want to. Crying has many benefits: It can allow you to release pent-up emotions, lower strain from challenging circumstances, and emotionally process your situation. This activity is particularly helpful for those who have trouble crying or don't feel safe doing so. By practicing crying in circumstances where you don't have a personal stake, you can lessen the pressure. Consult a physician or mental health provider before doing this if you are receiving treatment for, or have a history of, trauma.

1. Select a movie that you have watched before that makes you tear up or produces an urge to cry.

2. Watch the movie without outside distractions, in a place where you feel comfortable and safe.

3. When you notice your eyes water during a particularly emotional part of the movie, allow yourself to focus on the emotional content on-screen.

4. Inhale through your nose slowly and exhale through your mouth, and experience the emotions that arise from the movie.

5. Allow your breathing to return to normal as your eyes water.

6. When you notice yourself trying to push the tears down or stop crying, keep breathing and say to yourself, "It's okay to cry." Let your tears fall.

CHAPTER 2

Physical Self-Care

Cook a Love-and-Wellness Meal

ACTIVITY TIME:
3 hours

SUPPLIES:
Pen
Paper
Groceries

Comfort foods often have an association with childhood. It's not just eating that brings about this relationship; the memories of watching the food being gathered or shopped for, and the process of preparing, cooking, and eating the meal, create positive emotions. Emotions trigger the autonomic nervous system, so feelings like joy can slow your breathing and relax your body. Reliving these comfort meal experiences can be nourishing to your body, mind, and soul, making you feel cared for and safe at a visceral level. Think back to those times and try making it a practice once a week to enjoy a comfort food self-care experience. As you engage in this activity, savor each part of the process to create joy and the physical benefits it brings.

1. Write down some of the meals you ate as a child that bring back the best memories.

2. Circle the top three meals.

3. Put a star next to your favorite.

4. Identify the recipes and ingredients for that meal (it is okay to ask someone who remembers) and dedicate a shopping trip to gather what you need.

5. Wipe your calendar clear for your scheduled time of prepping, cooking, and eating.

6. Slowly and joyfully prepare the recipe.

7. Sit down and eat mindfully, engaging all your senses.

8. When done, text people who would have eaten this meal in the past to share a memory related to it, or recall past times spent with that person.

Catch the First Light

ACTIVITY TIME:
15 minutes

SUPPLIES:
Attire appropriate for
the temperature

Chair or blanket
(optional)

Although people spend more and more time online, they still long to connect with nature as their ancestors did. When you embrace the wonder of Mother Earth, you can take a childlike delight in the world around you. There is no more genuine expression of this than watching the sun rise from the east. There is something about experiencing first light that makes you feel ready for whatever happens throughout the rest of the day. From a scientific standpoint, getting fifteen minutes of sun per day has many benefits, including an influx of vitamin D that can lift your mood and support immune function.

1. Determine the best place near your home to watch the sunrise.

2. Look up the weather to figure out the next day with clear skies and determine the time of sunrise.

3. The night before, make sure you set your timer to wake you up in enough time to leisurely prepare to be at your spot fifteen minutes before sunrise; plan to get at least seven hours of sleep.

4. Set aside a folding chair or blanket to take with you, or search for a public bench when you arrive.

5. Experience the first light for at least fifteen minutes to get your daily dose of vitamin D.

A Simple Yoga Routine

ACTIVITY TIME:
5 minutes

SUPPLIES:
Device with internet access

Yoga mat or towel

People often carry kinks in their bodies. If you stop and pay attention to what your body is feeling, you may notice a tightness in your shoulders, a tenseness in your back, or a tingling in your legs, among other things. And although you know you need to do something, you might believe you don't have enough time to experience any improvement in how your body feels. Luckily, science has shined a light on yoga, demonstrating that just five minutes of this ancient practice can reduce the impact of the kinks and make you feel infinitely better.

1. If you have already practiced yoga, identify five poses you enjoy the most. If you are new to it, conduct a search for a "five-minute yoga class" video, and watch a few of them, picking five poses you like.

2. With your poses in mind, clear out a space in your living quarters with natural or soft lighting that is easy on the eyes.

3. Lay out a yoga mat or towel.

4. Follow the yoga routine for five minutes.

5. Focus on the experience of moving into the poses rather than the outcome.

6. Consider pairing this activity with a search on the origin and culture of yoga to honor its heritage.

Brunch in the Great Outdoors

ACTIVITY TIME:

3 hours

SUPPLIES:

Pen

Paper

Groceries

Picnic supplies

Outdoor cooking
supplies (if needed)

Being out in nature has been shown to help reduce cortisol levels, muscle tension, stress, and heart rate. What better way to support your physical self-care than by preparing and executing an outdoor brunch with loved ones where you can get the physical benefits of nature and the emotional benefits of spending time with people you care for? Your food and drinks menu can be as simple or gourmet as you like—what's important is that you enjoy uninterrupted time with friends or family in an outdoor environment where you can immerse yourself in the natural landscape.

1. Make up a list of three or four brunch guests.

2. Check the weather and figure out a day of the week that is most likely to be sunny.

3. Invite your guests and agree on a time and place to meet.

4. Create a menu and make a list of all the relevant ingredients.

5. Gather and prepare your brunch and picnic items. Feel free to invite others to bring items, too, and make a schedule for the event.

6. With the preparation complete, meet with your friends and unwind over a leisurely brunch, taking time to savor the landscape and sounds of nature.

7. Focus on the present moment and enjoy your conversation and the accompanying chemical boost in your body from bonding with others.

Crafting to Create

ACTIVITY TIME:
30 minutes

SUPPLIES:
Device with internet access

Craft supplies

Craft table or cleared surface

Whether you are engaged in work around the home, an office, or elsewhere, much of your time is likely spent completing tasks for others rather than being involved in creative expression. Crafting and making art have been found to have physical health benefits and can be important aspects of your self-care: Crafting can enhance dexterity, and creating art lowers blood pressure and cortisol. In this activity, I encourage you to take up a craft where you produce a useful object—especially one that you can use in your day-to-day life, like wall hangings, mugs, or scarves. Reconnect with your natural sense of creativity through crafting by selecting an activity that requires you to move your body (or hands) in different ways.

1. Browse an adult craft website, such as PureWow. Survey the available options for a usable creation, and select a craft that fits your interests and skill level.

2. Schedule into your calendar "Craft Time" so that you commit time for yourself.

3. Acquire the items on the list, and have them ready in advance of your crafting date.

4. Set up your workspace so that you are comfortable, the space is aesthetically pleasing, and supplies are accessible.

5. Begin your craft project, enjoy moving your body in a new way, and savor the sensations of relaxation in your body.

6. Start with one project a month and, as your abilities increase, devote more time.

Your Spa Ritual

ACTIVITY TIME:

2 hours

SUPPLIES:

Day pass at a spa

Book and magazines

Device to play music and
headphones

Women around the world and across cultures engage in bathing rituals. Whether these practices are for medicinal purposes, beautification, or socializing, they are underscored by the belief that caring for oneself is not an indulgence but rather a natural and necessary part of life. It is a way to refuel and tune into your body, develop a relationship with it, and give it what it needs. In this activity, you'll nourish yourself with a spa day, bringing the same level of attention to your experience that you give your job or other responsibilities. Many towns and cities have Korean, Russian, and Turkish baths where you can spend the day at a reasonable cost.

1. Clear several hours of a day on your calendar where you have no obligations or need for communication with others.

2. Select a day spa and buy a pass where you have access to baths, pampering treatments, and relaxation areas.

3. Inform significant others and family that you will be unavailable and will not have regular cell phone availability; you will call them if needed and respond to texts when you have breaks.

4. Obtain a variety of magazines and books you wish to read and unwind with.

5. Create a playlist of music that relaxes you and pack headphones.

6. Enjoy the day; luxuriate in the experience.

Mindful Walking Delights

ACTIVITY TIME:
15 minutes

SUPPLIES:
None

So often when people walk outside, they are talking on their cell phones or thinking about their upcoming duties. In fact, for some people, walking might feel more like one more chore, leading them to use their cars instead. Yet moving your body is one of the most beneficial activities for your physical and emotional well-being. In fact, the more physical activity you do, research indicates, the less fatigued you will feel. Imagine what it would feel like to slow down your walking moments and take in your surroundings. Tuning into your sensory experience like this encourages you to observe the present moment, disconnect from the concerns and stresses of life, and appreciate the beauty in the everyday scenes around you. You will likely find that the experience of getting from A to B brings you joy.

1. Pick a regular activity in your day that you can do by walking, like walking to the store to do an errand.

2. As you walk, engage your available senses, one at a time. What do you hear, see, feel, or smell?

3. Take a mental note of your physical sensations—for example, how the breeze feels on your face or what sound your shoes make on the ground.

4. Embrace and appreciate each day's unique sensual state as it influences your mood and well-being.

Savor the Wonder of Nature

ACTIVITY TIME:
30 minutes

SUPPLIES:
Phone or camera

Savoring is the act of allowing your senses to linger on an environment or experience to bring your full attention to it. Appreciating natural landscapes, for instance, has been found to strengthen immune health and lower blood pressure. One way to savor nature is to capture its beauty on camera by developing an outdoor photography hobby. When you start, just focus on enjoyment and creativity. There is no need to purchase tons of new or fancy equipment; use your phone's camera if you don't have a stand-alone camera at home. Consider taking a course, watching videos, or reading about photography to stimulate your creativity, which, coincidentally, also supports immune function.

1. Locate a local park or outdoor area with a walking path.

2. Pick a day to dedicate thirty minutes of your time to taking pictures and place it in your calendar.

3. On the appointed day, head to your destination.

4. Once there, take the first few minutes to savor the landscape by noticing the colors, shapes, and textures.

5. Determine whether you will photograph one specific category, such as flowers, or be more general, like landscapes.

6. Keep moving and shooting for at least twenty minutes.

7. At the end, create a digital photo album of your pictures and set it to music.

8. Watch the video whenever you need a boost.

Fun with Gardening

ACTIVITY TIME:

1 hour

SUPPLIES:

Planting bed container

Planting supplies and tools

Gloves

Tending to your own plants and garden can have physical benefits; research reveals that repotting plants leads to lower blood pressure and heart rate. It also reveals that people recuperating from illness in the hospital reported less pain when they had plants in their rooms. Gardening outdoors has been found to improve hand strength, and it also offers a daily dose of vitamin D. So dust off those gardening skills, engage in some prework on the internet, or talk to the professionals at your local nursery to determine which plants are best suited to your environment, climate, and experience level.

1. If you are new to this, focus on one type of plant that you wish to grow, such as a particular flower, herb, or vegetable.

2. Use a small or medium container and add soil to plant seeds or seedlings.

3. Pick a regular time to tend to your crop each day.

4. Take your time and focus your attention on watering and tending to your plants.

5. Notice how your body feels when tending to your plants. Observe whether you feel a sense of calm, relaxation, or connection. Notice whether your shoulders loosen or if you are moving your body more gently or purposefully as you cultivate.

Buddies in Nature

ACTIVITY TIME:
1 hour 30 minutes

SUPPLIES:
Phone with internet
  access

Stress impacts your body as well as your mind. It can contribute to chronic aches and pains, fatigue, heart conditions, and difficulty sleeping. This activity can help you address stress in your body. Just ninety minutes of walking in nature has been found to reduce stress. Moreover, as your body becomes accustomed to walking, the less fatigue you will feel. Create an opportunity to get these benefits by starting your nature walking habit. First, complete an easy internet search for accessible walking trails near your home. Next, find a hiking buddy or join a hiking club or other outdoor club to experience social benefits.

1. Determine what you would enjoy seeing in nature. This could be anything from certain types of birds if you are in a wooded area or wildflowers on a nature path.

2. Go through your contacts list and pick out the family or friends who you think would enjoy this adventure.

3. Pitch the idea to some people on the list and see what response you get: One "yes" is all you need.

4. Determine if and what you might want to "collect" and if you are collecting it by sight, photo, or actual object.

5. Pick a mutually agreeable time and place, and make sure there is a coffee shop nearby so you can discuss your experience and plan for the next time.

Body Brilliance

ACTIVITY TIME:
5 minutes

SUPPLIES:
None

Research has shown that when study participants experienced emotions, they felt corresponding sensations in specific parts of their bodies; this was similar across cultures. This data demonstrated what you likely already knew intuitively—that what affects your mind affects your body. When my clients have difficulty finding words to describe what they are going through or how they feel, I ask them to check in with themselves physically, give themselves comfort, and let their body provide insight into what they need in the moment. This activity will help you understand your needs by sourcing wisdom from your body. Over time, you will likely find that you do this naturally.

1. The next time you feel unsettled in your body, stop and notice the sensations.

2. Do a mental body scan by bringing your attention to the crown of your head and moving your awareness slowly down your body until you reach your feet.

3. Notice the one body part where you feel the most discomfort. Place your hand on that part of your body and gently rub it to provide comfort. If you cannot use your hands, simply bring your attention to the area.

4. Now ask that part of your body, "What message do you have for me?"

5. Pause and listen without judgment to what your body is telling you.

6. Take the action your body guided you to take.

Anoint Your Body

ACTIVITY TIME:
5 minutes

SUPPLIES:
Lotion or body oil

Often people become disconnected from their bodies and focus on them only for their utility, like getting from one place to the next or meeting the demands of the day. It is essential to develop a relationship with your body by giving it the same loving care and attention you would to other important people or things in your life. Self-massage is one way to do this. There are many benefits to massage and other forms of healing touch; they aid in relaxation and stress relief. This activity is an opportunity to reacquaint yourself with your body by lovingly touching it as you apply lotion or body oil.

1. If you have a favorite body oil or lotion, use it for this activity. Otherwise, purchase one with a great scent or a luxurious feel. Sample products to see what you like best.

2. After bathing, apply the body oil or lotion as you would typically, but do so slowly in circular motions or by gently sweeping the product up your skin.

3. Slow down whenever you notice yourself rushing, and remind yourself to focus on the experience rather than the time.

4. Take a mental note of how this experience feels and of moments of self-appreciation, such as "Wow, my shoulders are so strong" or "I love how soft my skin feels."

Dress from Your Soul

ACTIVITY TIME:
15 minutes

SUPPLIES:
Journal
Pen
Your wardrobe

The clothes you wear communicate a message to others. More importantly, your attire is a chance to celebrate and communicate your identity. Clothes don't "make" a woman, but they are a way a woman can express herself. Fashion trends and societal pressures can influence how you dress, robbing you of the freedom to explore, play, and have fun with clothes and accessories. Instead of fitting in with contemporary style, how about taking a soul-centered approach to your attire? For this activity, you'll take stock of the clothes in your closet and accessories in your drawer to allow yourself to express your inner you.

1. Take out your journal, and write a list of the ways you admire yourself or of characteristics that make you unique. If it's challenging, think about what others have told you they admire about you.

2. Ask yourself, "What outfit could I wear that embodies my uniqueness?"

3. Write what comes to mind without censoring yourself. Consider the colors, textures, and feel of those items.

4. Go to your closet, and identify pieces that match this newfound awareness. Touch each garment to notice what gives you a spark of pleasure or joy.

5. Put together an outfit, and consider going out for tea, taking a walk, or looking in the mirror to revel in your soul-centered attire.

6. Look for other ways to continue this in your daily dressing.

Child's Play

ACTIVITY TIME:
30 minutes

SUPPLIES:
Game supplies
(if needed)

Remember your childhood and recall your favorite games from gym class, recess, or the neighborhood. Those recollections likely bring a smile to your face, accompanied by lots of positive bubbling sensations in your body. When you played as a child, you were physically active but did not consider it to be exercise. Physical play and movement allow people to abandon the concerns of the day and be fully present in the moment. Moreover, when jumping double Dutch, playing tag, or spinning breathlessly with a Hula-Hoop, you are improving cardiovascular health, building stamina, and relieving the physical impact of stress. Playing games doesn't have to be reserved for childhood alone; you can bring that spirit into adulthood. This activity gives you permission to be a kid again by moving your body in play.

1. Think back to your favorite memories of physical play as a child, and pick one activity you can do alone or with a family member or friend.

2. Gather any necessary supplies, like a ball, rope, or chalk. Arrange a time to play and clear your schedule. Invite friends if you would like!

3. Play the game and enjoy yourself.

4. If you notice yourself looking at your watch or thinking about items on your to-do list, pause and bring your attention back to playing.

5. Compliment yourself and your partners on their great moves. At the end, share what you enjoyed most with one another.

Body Love

ACTIVITY TIME:
2 minutes

SUPPLIES:
Mirror

Each day, you take in multiple images of what an "ideal" body looks like. Although there is no one ideal, it takes effort to counteract the numerous messages about what a woman should look like. This can lead people to compare themselves to unrealistic standards or to versions of their bodies at an earlier point in their lives. This comes with a cost—lowering self-esteem and triggering stress and anxiety in (and about) their bodies. One way to counteract those messages and turn those impossible standards upside down is to practice a regular self-care ritual to honor the body you have right now. Because touch offers many benefits (e.g., stronger immune system, less depression and anxiety) here is an opportunity to pair words of affirmation with a loving touch.

1. Stand in front of a mirror that allows you to see as much of your body as possible.

2. Starting with the crown of your head, say aloud, "I love and honor you."

3. Place your hands over your ears, and say, "I love and honor you."

4. Rest your hands lightly over your face, and repeat the phrase.

5. Move to your shoulders, then torso, then arms while speaking the phrase.

6. Continue to each major body part until you reach your feet. If there are any body parts you cannot reach, bring your attention to each one while repeating your phrase.

Move Like a Queen

ACTIVITY TIME:
2 minutes

SUPPLIES:
None

Have you ever noticed that when your mood is low, your body captures the energy of those emotions? For example, you may find your body slouched or hunched over when you feel sad. By contrast, when your mood is elevated, your body is likely to be open, your chin up and shoulders back, reflecting this positive mood. Research demonstrates that assuming a particular stance called the "power pose" can help you feel like you are ready to take on the world. In other words, you can feel more confident and able to confront the challenges ahead by moving your body in a certain way. In this activity, you will practice purposeful movement to help you tap into your sense of confidence and self-worth.

1. Find an open space long enough for you to move about twenty feet. Stand straight with your chin parallel to the floor, and place your gaze softly on an image about twenty feet ahead.

2. Raise your shoulders, bringing them up and back toward your back.

3. Step forward with your dominant leg and move into a stroll.

4. As you walk with your eyes focused ahead, form a gentle smile by turning the corners of your lips up.

5. Move forward until you reach your destination; notice how good your body feels.

6. Consider reciting a positive affirmation (e.g., "I am powerful and purposeful.") as you step forward, to bring even more confidence to your movement.

Problem-Solving with Movement

ACTIVITY TIME:
15 minutes

SUPPLIES:
Journal or paper
Pen
Device to play music

People face daily challenges that require them to find solutions. You may be conditioned to believe that the way to find a solution is to power through your emotions, think it through, and figure it out by sheer force of will. But another option is to engage your body in the solution-finding process; after all, one of the benefits of physical activity is problem-solving. So, for this activity, you'll move purposefully and activate your body, and, at the same time, set the intention that a solution will come once you have some distance from thinking about it.

1. Think about the situation or problem you are trying to solve.

2. Write it in your journal or on a piece of paper, and put it aside.

3. Turn on the radio or streaming music service to your favorite station or playlist.

4. Play your music, and move your body freely.

5. Raise your arms, and gently move them like a conductor leading an orchestra.

6. Each time you extend your arms, open your hands and grasp the air, making a fist as you imagine you are grabbing pieces of information that will help you solve the problem.

7. After ten minutes, go back to your paper and write any solutions.

Line Dance Your Way to Fun

ACTIVITY TIME:
20 minutes

SUPPLIES:
Device with internet
 access

Dancing, like other forms of physical activity, improves cardiovascular health, supports your musculoskeletal system, and aids in the prevention and treatment of chronic disease. Across the world, social or line dances have a particularly positive social benefit and are a great way to incorporate physical activity. These dances create shared experiences of fun, collaboration, and movement. Learn the latest dances solo so you can break them out on the dance floor at your next gathering, or even expose others to a new dance.

1. Do an internet search using the phrase "popular line dance," and insert either the year or region of the country or world you are in.

2. Review a few videos, and choose the one you like best.

3. Watch it once without trying to replicate the moves. Watch again, and slowly practice the moves.

4. On the third viewing, attempt to master the dance. Focus on grasping the first third of the dance, and continue in thirds until you have a basic grasp of the full routine.

5. Give yourself permission to focus on fun rather than perfection; think of it as a dress rehearsal, and try to dance for twenty to thirty minutes to get the most benefit.

6. At your last viewing, get into it and do the dance to the best of your ability.

Treasure Hunt

ACTIVITY TIME:
30 minutes

SUPPLIES:
Money ($10)
Timer
Activity Tracker

Your body requires movement, yet many people have lives where they spend little time moving throughout the day. Lack of movement can contribute to many challenges for your body and can place a good deal of stress on your systems. By contrast, activities such as walking briskly and regularly can help lower stress and support your mental and physical health. Even though modern life does not incentivize movement, you can find joyful ways to move in your daily life. In this activity, you'll have an adventure and add some movement to your day.

1. Assemble a small group of friends, and invite them to walk with you on a treasure hunt at a mall or shopping strip.

2. Upon arrival, tell your friends that you each have $10 and thirty minutes to wander around and find the most unique treasure you can find within your budget.

3. Agree that the winner will be the person with the most unique item and the most activity on their tracker.

4. Set a timer, coordinate watches, and agree to return to your starting location within the allotted time. Go!

5. When you identify your treasure, purchase it, and return to the starting point.

6. When everyone has returned, review the items and the number of activity steps for each person, and declare a winner.

Body Love Tech Break

ACTIVITY TIME:

10 minutes

SUPPLIES:

Device with internet access

Timer

Water

Magazine

As counterintuitive as it may seem, you can use technology to counter the impact of technology. When you sit in front of your computer screens, tablets, or phones, you can get lost in a world of digital distractions and lose track of time for hours on end. But your body was not designed to sit and stare endlessly, and you are, by nature, a moving machine that thrives on refreshment and novelty. Luckily, you can use your devices to schedule reminders to step away from your screens, move and replenish your body, and enjoy the present moment in the real world. Try this activity when you know you will have a long period of screen time, whether it's during work or leisure hours.

1. Conduct a search for three simple stretches that address the three areas of your body that most commonly hold stress.

2. Get a physical coffee table book or magazine with pictures of one of your favorite subjects. It could be art, fashion, sports, architecture, or anything that delights you.

3. Set a reminder on your timer to ring at 0:50 of every hour of anticipated screen time.

4. When it rings, move away from your screen, and breathe in deeply for five seconds, hold for five seconds, and breathe out for five seconds. Do this for a few rounds.

5. Do your three stretches.

6. For the rest of the ten minutes, sit and sip your water while leafing through your book or magazine.

CHAPTER 3

Mental
Self-Care

Clearing a Mental Path

ACTIVITY TIME:
10 minutes

SUPPLIES:
Journal

Pen

Sometimes, to begin engaging in regular self-care, it takes shifting your mindset about its importance and how it will benefit your life. The goal is to bring out the challenges to creating a more robust self-care life, create a vision of the pluses of incorporating more self-care, build in accountability, and think of inspired self-care actions. This will help you prepare to change your behavior in ways that have a positive impact on your well-being. Think of this activity as mentally clearing the path.

1. Take out your journal and write each of the following questions on a blank sheet of paper:

    a) What is the cost of not prioritizing my self-care?

    b) What barriers do I face that keep me from focusing on self-care?

    c) What would my life be like if I practiced more self-care? How will I feel?

    d) How would others in my life be positively influenced by my self-care?

    e) Who in my life can either partner with me or help keep me accountable for prioritizing my self-care?

    f) What one action can I commit to today to prioritize my self-care?

2. Take the action you are led to take. Revisit these questions often, and add any new insights.

Calming Meditation

ACTIVITY TIME:
15 minutes

SUPPLIES:
Timer

Overwhelming scientific evidence attests to the numerous benefits of meditation: stress reduction, enhanced well-being, creativity, and mind clearing. It is one of the least expensive commitments you can make to yourself that pays off in dividends repeatedly. Meditation takes a minimal time commitment to execute but requires a consistent commitment to maximize its impact. Making it a priority in your daily life is an important act of self-care. Still, even with all the known benefits of meditation, it can be challenging to practice, especially in the beginning. Repeating a phrase can ease you into practicing. Feel free to start with five minutes and work up to fifteen.

1. Find a quiet space to turn out the lights and sit comfortably without interruption for fifteen minutes.

2. Set the alarm on your watch or phone for fifteen minutes, and turn off all other notifications on this device.

3. Close your eyes and imagine yourself in the safest and most supportive place you have ever been.

4. Envision as many elements of that space as you can: What do you hear? What do you smell? What do you feel? What do you see?

5. Once you are immersed in the image, repeat the phrase "I am [pause for two seconds] relaxed [pause for two seconds]" over and over, slowly and silently.

6. Continue until the alarm goes off.

The Golden Breath

ACTIVITY TIME:
2 minutes

SUPPLIES:
None

The ability to breathe is a splendid human phenomenon. Breathing is both involuntary and voluntary and is essential to living. Many people don't know that if they take the time to explore their breath, it can have a tremendous impact on the quality of their lives. Breathing with purpose and intention can help you process emotions, regulate your nervous system, and tap into your inner wisdom and strength. Because the body and mind are connected, you can use this activity (alone or with others) to calm your mind, get clarity, or strengthen your mental resolve.

1. Sit in a relaxing space.

2. Inhale deeply through your nose, then exhale out of your mouth.

3. On your next inhalation, imagine the air around you as a golden mist, with every breath coming into your body moving from your head to your toes.

4. Imagine the mist contains the qualities of gold: high value, resilient, and strong.

5. When the mist reaches your toes, hold your breath for a second or two and then slowly release.

6. Count while doing so, and as you become more adept, aim for a five- to seven-second exhale.

7. Repeat at least seven times, and notice the peace, calm, and resolve you bring into the rest of the day.

Daily Gratitude Journal

ACTIVITY TIME:

10 minutes

SUPPLIES:

Notes app on your phone or journal or paper and pen

Paying more attention to the little things that positively affect you during the day enhances happiness and well-being in life. Paying attention is the first step, but acknowledging, reflecting on, appreciating, and feeling grateful for those experiences transforms episodic happiness into long-lasting joy. A term for this practice is *savoring*: giving yourself the opportunity to digest and revel in your experiences. When you deepen your savoring skills, you counterbalance your brain's tendency to spot and linger on the negative, and you develop new neural pathways to seek and hold on to the positive. This activity offers the building blocks for creating a gratitude practice and can be paired with the Wind Down with Gratitude activity (page 15).

1. Create a heading on your phone (or a piece of paper or journal) called "Today's Gratitude."

2. During the day, whenever something happens to you that makes you feel good about yourself or someone in whom you are invested, add that to the list of Today's Gratitude.

3. Repeat this exercise every day for a week.

4. At the end of the week, read your lists, reflect on any themes, and note any shift in your ability to notice positive experiences.

5. Check in to see if you would be willing to continue for thirty days. If so, proceed.

Explore New Worlds

ACTIVITY TIME:
1 hour

SUPPLIES:
Library card

Taking a trip to the library as a child was a special activity. It was like a physical treasure hunt for your curiosity. Walking down the aisles and reading the titles as you went by was like seeing hidden clues to new worlds. As you did this, you likely expanded your mind and opened yourself to dreaming about the possibilities life holds. Recalling positive childhood memories is an act of mental self-care; doing so has been linked to positive mental health and well-being. Adding a physical reenactment of your childhood library trips can magnify the impact. A library trip involves so much more bodily involvement than an internet search. Walking through the library stimulates many of your senses, and the feeling of finding just the right book is just not the same in an online search.

1. Go to your local public library. Stroll through the aisles until you find a subject that interests you.

2. Slow down, and start to peruse the titles of the books in the aisle until one or two call your attention.

3. Take them to a table, sit down, and flip through them.

4. If they satisfy that initial attention grab, take them to the front desk and check them out (or keep looking until you find something).

5. Consider taking more time by going to a coffee shop and savoring reading as well as reawakening your childlike awe.

Scheduling Me Time

ACTIVITY TIME:
20 minutes

SUPPLIES:
Internet access
Weekly calendar

Although many people crave more time to do the things they enjoy, people often don't know when or how to fit them into their schedules. A helpful first step is to take inventory of how you are spending your time. When most of your time is spent in activities not of your choosing, it can lead to resentment and associated negative automatic thoughts, such as *My time belongs to others*, that can contribute to mental and emotional stress. Ease the mental strain by purposefully planning and practicing activities you enjoy. It will pave the way for positive thoughts and the lowered cortisol level that comes from such thoughts.

1. Download a copy of the weekly calendar from the book section of my website CicelyBrathwaite .com/books.

2. For a week, in as great detail as you can, write down how you spent your time for each hour that you're awake.

3. At week's end, review the list, and place each item into these color-coded categories: "Things I had to do," "Things that are good for me," "Things that are unnecessary," and "Things I enjoy."

4. Determine which category you grant the most time. Plan your schedule for the next week and consciously add 10 percent more time to the "Things you Enjoy" category, and remove 10 percent of the time previously devoted to unnecessary items. Enjoy your week and notice the positive thoughts you create with this new focus.

A Whole New World

ACTIVITY TIME:
Variable

SUPPLIES:
Course registration fees (if applicable)

Relevant course supplies

Learning something new benefits your brain no matter what stage of womanhood you are in. Neuroplasticity refers to the fact that the human brain can develop new neural pathways throughout the life span. Previously, scientists believed brains only developed through late adolescence and early adulthood. Now scientists know that people not only strengthen their mental capacity throughout their life span, but that it is especially important to challenge yourself mentally as you age to support a healthy aging process and cognitive ability. Public libraries and community centers are wonderful places to get exposed to new ideas, especially since they often offer free or low-cost courses and seminars. Expand your mind by enrolling in an offering that is a bit (or a lot) out of your comfort zone.

1. Visit your local public library or community center and inquire about the in-person and online classes and seminars they offer.

2. Be open to the opportunity to pursue a childhood talent that has been dormant or a topic that sounds intriguing.

3. Enroll in a course or seminar (e.g., language, art, music, or history) that lights up your heart and mind *and* meets at a time that fits your schedule.

4. Make the commitment, and enjoy taking the time to develop your mind and experience yourself in a different light.

5. Allow yourself to have a learning curve with no pressure and no judgment.

Less Is More

ACTIVITY TIME:
2 hours

SUPPLIES:
Nondigital reading materials (e.g., books, magazines)

Less is more. People say that about many different things, and in the case of stimuli, nothing could be closer to the truth. Each moment, people receive far more stimuli than they can process. This flooding of information means that every part of your system is overwhelmed with noise, leaving very little free space in your mind. It can be a challenge to quiet your mind once you've been in "go mode" all day. This two-pronged activity provides a wind-down by reading, followed by quiet time in your home or nature. I recommend practicing this activity once a week when you can take two hours for yourself.

1. Block out two hours either in the morning when you wake up or in the evening before you typically sleep.

2. Silence your phone, and do not turn on your computer, television, or radio.

3. Read something that comes in physical form, like a book, magazine, or newspaper.

4. Create a non-digital routine: Connect to your thoughts, previewing or reviewing the day; connect to your goals for the day; and connect to your physical environment either inside or outside.

5. Enjoy the silence or make your own music by singing or humming to yourself.

6. Take your heartbeat old-school style by putting your fingers on your pulse or the veins in your neck, and notice how slow your heartbeat is.

Read Differently

ACTIVITY TIME:
10 minutes

SUPPLIES:
Book

Reading keeps your brain active; in fact, it has been described as exercise for your brain. In that sense, the more you read, the more you strengthen the brain areas and functions activated when you read. Your concentration, comprehension, and memory expand through reading. When you read something different from that which you would typically choose, you create new neural pathways that are helpful at any point in life but particularly as you age. In addition, exposing yourself to new perspectives and ideas through nonfiction can increase your awareness, critical thinking, and compassion for the circumstances in other people's lives. This activity aids the learning process, so support your brain and expand your horizons with a new habit of learning new information.

1. Identify a topic or person you would like to learn more about, and search for and obtain a related nonfiction book.

2. Read five pages of the book every day. Feel free to read more, but commit to reading at least five pages daily. Read while taking public transportation, or read as part of your morning or bedtime ritual.

3. Consider the insights and new learning you gain each day, and see what connections you make between that learning and other areas in your life.

4. Share your insights with a loved one or friends to continue processing your new learning and deepening your insights.

Conscious Uncoupling

ACTIVITY TIME:

15 minutes

SUPPLIES:

Paper

Pen

Chronic multitasking impacts brain development and, over time, can impair decision-making and emotional control. A significant catalyst for multitasking is the beautifully crafted handheld supercomputer you hold in your hands. When you focus on one activity at a time, you can give that task the full attention it deserves, thus allowing you to be more present and strengthen your attention and concentration. As you work to develop a habit, start here by focusing on your phone as a multitasking culprit. See how this compares to your experience with Narrate Your Life (page 66) later on in the book.

1. For one week, write down when you reach for your phone or other device while engaged in another activity. You don't need to record every time, but try to capture a general picture of whether you looked at your phone while eating or while spending time with loved ones, for example.

2. At the end of the week, review your list, and see which activities are on it.

3. Start with the activity where you multitasked (reached for your phone) least.

4. In week 2, starting with the least multitasked activity, put your phone away before beginning the activity. When you have the urge to pick up your phone or do so without thinking, tell yourself, "Let it go."

5. Continue until you have uncoupled this activity from the phone. Build on this uncoupling by moving to other activities.

Brain Food Taco

ACTIVITY TIME:
20 minutes

SUPPLIES:
Groceries

The food you eat for breakfast sets the stage for the rest of your day. When you start your day with brain foods, and the foods that help your blood sugar remain stable, you support your ability to concentrate and think clearly. You may find that focusing on making the meal becomes a type of mindful meditation that sets you up to start the day with a clearer head. I have suggested a menu to get your creativity flowing, but try to use fresh vegetables, whole grains, and lean proteins.

1. Prepare the night before to make a breakfast taco. Get 2 small corn tortillas, 1 cup of spinach, and 2 eggs, and put them aside in the refrigerator. Bake 4 ounces of salmon (with your favorite spices), and then put it in an airtight container with a tablespoon of olive oil on top.

2. In the morning, sauté the spinach with your favorite seasonings and then add the eggs and scramble.

3. Heat your salmon to warm it up, and cut it finely.

4. Prepare your tacos with your favorite dressing (e.g., salsa, crema, Greek yogurt), put the ingredients inside, and munch away as your brain says "thank you."

Joyful Morning Routine

ACTIVITY TIME:
5 minutes

SUPPLIES:
None

Merriam-Webster defines joy as "the emotion evoked by well-being, success, or good fortune or by the prospect of possessing what one desires." It is easy to recognize joy when something monumental happens, but it can exist equally in small and medium experiences you already enjoy. How you begin your day sets the tone for the hours that follow. Seeking, practicing, and prioritizing joy every morning is helpful for your mind, body, and soul, but it takes practice and patience. What you will likely experience is that you strengthen resilience by balancing the challenges of your life with pockets of joy. This activity is meant to help you notice and create moments of joy in your life, even in the mundane.

1. In the morning, look over the major activities on your to-do list for the day.

2. Notice which ones hold the possibility of joyful moments. For instance, while you are providing caretaking for a loved one, might there be joy in the moment of connection you feel?

3. Pick one activity, and mentally forecast a moment of joy that you will create during that time.

4. When the time comes, bring the element of joy you rehearsed to that situation.

5. Notice how you feel after creating the joyful moment.

6. As you practice this activity in the future, increase the number of joyful moments you create each day.

Ask the Question

ACTIVITY TIME:

10 minutes

SUPPLIES:

Journal

Pen

There are many reasons why you might feel worried or anxious, some due to biological factors and others due to the realities of modern life. If you often experience these feelings, and they affect your ability to function daily, or if the thoughts feel out of control, it could be time to enlist the support of a mental health professional before trying this activity. Triggers for worry and anxiety may arise when you are dealing with something new, something that's out of your control, or when you have emotions you have not yet uncovered. Practicing using your mind to uncover the roots of your discomfort can help ease your emotions and lessen worry and anxiety. This activity provides a road map for doing so.

1. The next time you feel worry or anxiety, notice it and ask, "What is going on?"

2. Write the answer that comes to mind without editing yourself. Feel free to write words or phrases rather than complete sentences.

3. Pause, and notice any shifts in your worry to see if you feel calmer.

4. Ask the question several times, and record your answers until you know what contributes to your worry.

5. Once you've identified what's worrying you, ask yourself, "What's in my control that would shift this situation?"

6. Notice whether there is an action to take (and take it) or whether doing the exercise was enough to lessen your worry.

I Am Worthy

ACTIVITY TIME:
30 minutes

SUPPLIES:
Phone for music

Paper

Pen

Self-worth is broadly defined as "a deep sense of knowing that you have inherent value by virtue of being alive, which is not contingent on the opinions of others." There are many cultural messages of how a woman "should" be or look that create a narrow view of womanhood that can erode self-worth. Positive self-worth helps people develop a mental inner ally to squash their inner critic and actively refute negative messages. It requires practice to cultivate self-worth. In this activity, you'll strengthen your worthiness muscles by listing all the reasons you are worthy.

1. Set the mood by selecting songs that encourage self-celebration. "I'm Beautiful" by Bette Midler is a great place to start.

2. Take out your paper and pen, and write a list of fifty reasons you are FABULOUS. As you generate ideas, draw from your attributes, accomplishments, and aspirations.

3. If you feel stuck, move to things others have told you about how you have helped/benefited/cared for/affected them.

4. Return to things you know about yourself.

5. Give yourself permission to return to the list if you have difficulty generating fifty reasons at one time. Place it on your calendar and set a date with yourself.

6. Once you finish, place the list somewhere you can see and read it often.

Release the ANTs

ACTIVITY TIME:
10 minutes

SUPPLIES:
Paper
Pen

Dr. Daniel Amen popularized the acronym *ANTs* to describe the automatic negative thoughts many people experience as part of daily living. Such thoughts can run rampant in your mind, negatively influence how you see yourself, and affect your brain and body because of the chemicals the brain secretes when you have negative thoughts. This activity is inspired by a cognitive behavioral technique to help bring awareness to unexamined thoughts to lessen their hold.

1. Write a list of the most common ANTs that you experience. For example, *I won't succeed* or *People don't like me.*

2. On a separate piece of paper, create three columns, and give each column the following headline: ANT, Reminder, Counterstatement.

3. In the ANT column, write one of your most common ANTs.

4. Before moving to the Reminder column, visualize a red stop sign to help you refrain from focusing on your ANT.

5. In the Reminder section, write a statement of self-compassion, such as "It's just a thought. I am in the process of accepting all that is wonderful about me and my flaws."

6. In the Counterstatement column, write a more accurate statement to combat your ANT, such as "Sometimes I will succeed, sometimes I will fail. Success is a process."

7. Practice this the next time you have an ANT.

Fixation Point

ACTIVITY TIME:
1 minute

SUPPLIES:
Photo
Timer

Do you ever find yourself mired in negative thoughts, unable to escape them easily? One way to make an escape and care for yourself mentally is to purposefully create positive emotional experiences to influence your mood and mind. In this activity, you'll create a positive emotional state by gazing at a photo of someone you associate with positive emotions. This action will bring the happy emotions to the present and can give you the same benefits (e.g., lowered stress, more joyful mood) as if you were in their presence. This exercise is a riff on the work of folks at HeartMath, a wonderful resource you can find in the Resources section (page 117).

1. Find a comfortable place to sit with no distractions.

2. Adjust your body until you feel comfortable.

3. Select a photo of a loved one, pet, or public figure you admire that brings about positive feelings.

4. Set the alarm for one minute.

5. Fix your gaze on the photo, breathe gently and evenly, and allow your positive feelings to flow.

6. If you notice that you've become distracted, bring your attention back to the photo.

7. When the timer rings, turn it off and continue your day.

8. Once you learn to sit quietly for a minute, consider adding thirty- to sixty-second increments each week until you reach five minutes.

Solve Something

ACTIVITY TIME:
20 minutes

SUPPLIES:
Children's puzzle books

Pencil

There is abundant evidence that women engage in a lot of unaccounted-for labor. With all that you carry in your mind about what needs to be done, people you need to care for, or problems you need to resolve, it can be challenging to turn your thoughts off long enough to relax. Puzzles can help. Solving puzzles can enhance visual-spatial skills, lower stress, and improve mood through release of dopamine, which is known as the "happy hormone." For this activity, you'll use children's puzzles because they are easier and won't cause frustration when trying to solve them; you can just focus on the experience.

1. Do an internet search for "kids' puzzle books" and purchase one or two.

2. Once you have the books, schedule a time to do some of the exercises.

3. At the appointed time, take out the books and plan to solve at least five puzzles. Before starting, rate your stress level on a scale from 0 (low) to 10 (high).

4. If, after completing five puzzles, you'd like to continue, do so.

5. Enjoy the sense of accomplishment, release, and singular focus.

6. Once you are done, rate your mood again, and notice whether there have been any shifts. If you notice less stress, pick one relaxing self-care activity from the book to help you continue winding down.

Bedtime Routine

ACTIVITY TIME:

1 hour

SUPPLIES:

Alarm

Book (optional)

Device to play music/
playlist (optional)

Journal and pen
(optional)

Regular high-quality sleep has many benefits: It supports your brain function, mood, concentration, and ability to make decisions. Nonetheless, sometimes there are factors outside of your control that impact your ability to practice good sleep hygiene. But what is within your control is taking your sleep practices seriously so that you give yourself the best opportunity to get good sleep. A precursor to good sleep is having a strong bedtime routine that helps prime you to fall asleep more easily and clear the impacts of the day from your body and mind.

1. Set a reminder on your phone to get ready for bed about one hour before bedtime.

2. When the reminder chimes, start your evening routine before putting on your pajamas.

3. Orient your mind toward winding down by engaging in a winding-down activity like listening to a soothing playlist, journaling, or reading a book. Aim for an activity without screens.

4. Once you get tired, stop the activity, turn off the lights, and go to sleep.

5. If you have trouble sleeping because your mind is wandering, permit yourself not to follow those thoughts by letting them float out of your mind rather than hold your attention. Instead, focus on your breathing until you drift off to sleep.

6. If you don't fall asleep after a while, get out of bed, and return to your soothing activity until you are tired again.

Narrate Your Life

ACTIVITY TIME:
5 minutes

SUPPLIES:
None

At times, you might find yourself engaging in activities to keep yourself from feeling your emotions, or coping with things that don't feel quite right. One of the ways this might show up is by engaging in distracting behaviors. It's essential to recognize that those behaviors are simply a way of trying to take care of yourself; so rather than judge yourself, be compassionate. Distracting behaviors include snacking when not hungry, scrolling on social media, or binge-watching shows. Rather than focus on what you are not doing, it's helpful to notice what you are doing and to explore your underlying needs so that you can meet them.

1. The next time you find yourself engaged in a loop of a distracting behavior, pause, notice it, and say, "I'm trying to distract myself."

2. Bring curiosity to your experience, and ask, "What do I need right now?"

3. Once you receive your answer, ask, "Is this giving me what I need, or do I need something else? If the answer is yes, continue with the behavior; otherwise, move to step 4. For example, you might need a soothing shower, hydration, rest, a hug, a good cry, some journal reflection, a talk with a friend, or some exercise.

4. Ask, "Is it okay to give myself what I really need?" If the answer is yes, act on your need.

5. If the answer is no, continue what you were doing without judgment and revisit this exercise next time.

Lighten the Load

ACTIVITY TIME:
15 minutes

SUPPLIES:
Phone calendar

Did you ever notice that your mood is brighter after a good old spring-cleaning? It turns out that researchers have identified a link between clutter and mood. Clutter is, simply put, a collection of items that are spread out, disorganized, or messy that either don't have, or aren't in, an assigned location. Studies show that people with more clutter surrounding them feel more negatively about themselves and the world and are less satisfied with their lives. Address the clutter and lighten your load. Although it might not be feasible for you to spend hours decluttering, you can start a little at a time. Your clutter wasn't created in a day, so give yourself time to go through the process.

1. Pick a time of day when you can commit fifteen minutes to declutter for the next two weeks, and set a reoccurring reminder in your calendar.

2. Each day, pick one small section of your living space, and focus on decluttering just that area.

3. Sort items into "keep" and "don't keep" piles.

4. At the end of the fifteen-minute session, finish what you're doing, and notice how it feels to declutter the space.

5. Once a week, take away the items that you are giving away. Items that you are throwing away can be taken out on trash day.

CHAPTER 4

Social Self-Care

Organize Your Inbox

ACTIVITY TIME:
25 minutes

SUPPLIES:
Device with internet access

Research shows that email inbox clutter may affect you in a way similar to having physical clutter in your home. To make time for social self-care and have the wherewithal to deepen your social ties, you need to first clear out situations in your life that contribute to emotional clutter. Whereas some people relish organizing, many people find it tiring and stressful. That's why it can be helpful to set aside small chunks of time to chip away at the decluttering and to celebrate your progress as you go.

1. Set aside twenty-five minutes on your calendar when you can be undisturbed, and select your favorite upbeat music playlist.

2. Start by deleting all your junk emails.

3. Clap your hands once you finish.

4. Go through all the emails that have been unopened and are more than a year old, and delete them.

5. Again, clap your hands.

6. Now look at all emails that have been opened and are a year old, and delete them as well.

7. Once again, clap.

8. With the remainder of the emails, start from the top, make categories for them, and put them in their correct places.

9. When the twenty-five minutes are up, stand up, and give yourself a standing ovation. Repeat this process once a week until your inbox is organized.

Paying It Forward

ACTIVITY TIME:
Varied

SUPPLIES:
Device with internet
access

Strong evidence suggests that volunteering is as beneficial for volunteers as it is for the recipient of the acts of service. Volunteering is a form of self-care that can deepen compassion and meaning and can also lower the strain associated with stressors, lower depression, enhance feelings of connection, and boost moods. When you couple volunteering with social interaction through group volunteer efforts, you are contributing to your well-being in magnificent ways. It is a form of social self-care in that you are enhancing your sense of community. A group working together can do much to improve the conditions within the community and in the world.

1. Identify a cause you feel passionate about supporting (e.g., children's sports, a particular disease or health condition) or a group whose efforts you want to aid (e.g., a social justice cause, a local club or organization)

2. Once you have identified the cause, browse the internet, and determine where there are volunteer prospects in your local area to connect with. Contact them to see where you can plug into their efforts. Make sure to ask for opportunities that allow you to interact with other volunteers or organizers or provide direct service to people.

3. Once you've secured a volunteer spot, enjoy yourself, and interact with other volunteers.

4. Record your efforts, and share them on your social media platforms or with friends so that others may be inspired.

Shared Activity Fellowship

ACTIVITY TIME:
3 hours

SUPPLIES:
Varied, based on the activity selected

Busy schedules can make it easy for weeks or months to go by without spending time with some of the people you enjoy the most. It can be helpful to have a reoccurring date and preplanned activity on the calendar to help keep these relationships a priority. The folks at my husband's social club have a regularly scheduled Monday-night poker game with a core group every week and a rotating cast that drops by often. You can pick the frequency that works for you and your friends, whether that's weekly, biweekly, monthly, or something else. The important thing is to pick a realistic schedule and a shared activity to take the pressure off having to plan something new each time.

1. Make a list of the people you'd like to get together with on a regular basis.

2. Think of some activities that everyone on your list might enjoy—for example, board games, salsa dancing, old movies, book club, or cooking.

3. Reach out to the group with your suggestions for activities and scheduling (how often and on which day of the week or month the group will meet).

4. Create a list of rotating hosts for these soirees so you can share the responsibility of hosting.

5. If necessary, agree upon a budget and dues to share the financial burdens among the group.

6. Enjoy the ongoing fellowship.

Taking a Well Day

ACTIVITY TIME:
6 hours

SUPPLIES:
None

Moving out of your daily patterns, taking a break from the pressures, and focusing on fun can create memorable, perhaps even magical, experiences with others and joy in your life. For this activity, forgo your typical routine as you would on a sick day. But because this is a well day, instead of resting, prioritize spontaneity and fun. This activity is great for when you need a mood boost or when you are craving the company of others. It can be especially important if your regular routine keeps you isolated from others. If you are unable to find someone to spend time with you on that day, being out in public and in the company of others can yield similar benefits.

1. Check the weather and ensure that it will be a splendid day.

2. Call around to determine whether you can find a crew to share the day with or whether this will be a solo activity out in public.

3. Call into work and tell them you are taking a sick day (or plan a personal day if that aligns more with your values/company policy).

4. Decide to do at least two or three things that have been on your fun list but that you haven't gotten around to.

5. Leave the house early and do them, but also leave yourself open to unexpected fun.

6. Take photos with your phone throughout the day to chronicle your fun. If it is a solo day, share the photos with friends later.

Date Night

ACTIVITY TIME:
3 hours

SUPPLIES:
Date-night outfits

It is easy to fall into a routine that, upon closer inspection, can seem like a rut. Long-term relationships can feel stifling even when you enjoy each other's company, so this activity is for you. Tending to your romantic relationships is an important part of your social self-care and can enhance intimacy in the relationship. It's nice to remember the energy that went into planning dates when the relationship was just starting and blossoming. The attention and effort you paid to the early-stage relationship can be helpful even now when it has been ongoing for a while. Recapturing that energy can jump-start a new season of excitement and novelty into your relationship and help you bond and deepen intimacy. After one round, you can decide whether to continue as is or start creating new date-night ideas. It's time to reinvigorate date night.

1. Flip a coin to determine who will plan (and then you can alternate) the first date night.

2. Whoever's turn it is will plan to re-create one of the best moments of your early dating period.

3. Give yourself a much more generous budget than your previous date.

4. Go out and enjoy yourselves.

Pin the Tale on a Fantasy Vacation

ACTIVITY TIME:
30 minutes

SUPPLIES:
Large map
Pen
Blindfold

Taking vacations can have many mental health benefits, especially when they are well planned, not overscheduled, and focused on joy and wonder. Research reveals that planning a vacation reduces stress, leads to more motivation, and aids cardiovascular health by lowering the risk of heart disease. You can extend these benefits and experience added vacation joy and interest by including a partner or close friend. The idea here is to allow mystery and magic to play a part in your planning and execution of this magical mystery tour.

1. With a friend or partner, place a large map on a wall, and circle all the destinations you want to visit.

2. One of you should wear a blindfold, hold the pen, and spin around while the other person guides the spinning person toward the map to mark it.

3. The circled destination closest to the mark will be your next vacation destination.

4. Start planning details of your trip together by sharing ideas of exciting, relaxing, and fun elements of your trip.

5. Share photos or articles about your destination. Prepare meals and beverages inspired by your location to build excitement. Book flights, lodging, and fun excursions.

6. Enjoy the ride, and when you arrive, dance and party throughout the days.

Grown-ups Need Friends, Too

ACTIVITY TIME:
10 minutes

SUPPLIES:
Phone

School provides many opportunities to create relationships, whether out of necessity so you don't eat lunch alone in the cafeteria or out of shared interests, like theater or sports. Adulthood is different, especially if your schedule is jam-packed with life responsibilities. Seeing friends can feel like another obligation. But friendship is just as important in adulthood as it is in childhood, so although you might not have the same easy access to friends, moving them up on your priority list is important. When you do, you will likely find that friendships boost your mood. In fact, research supports the fact that they also boost your immune function and overall health. So, practice building grown-up friendships.

1. Open your contact list in your phone and pick one person from the list you'd like to know better.

2. Brainstorm an activity you think you might both enjoy. For example, you both might enjoy thrifting or a particular type of coffee or tea.

3. Invite the person to participate in that activity. Once you've agreed on the date, go out and enjoy yourself.

4. Send a short, follow-up text later that day to tell the person how much you enjoyed their company.

5. The following week, send an email (or DM) with a link to an article, video, or compelling fact related to your shared interest with the subject "Thought of you when I saw this."

6. If the person matches your enthusiasm and you are enjoying their company, continue the process.

Couple Support Network

ACTIVITY TIME:
2 hours

SUPPLIES:
None

All relationships go through stages, and each stage has its joys and struggles. Gaining perspective, envisioning what a shared future outside of a rough patch might look like, and reminding yourselves what led you to first commit to each other can be strengthening exercises for any couple. Even if your relationship feels solid, continuing to make it a priority and staying open to new areas of growth is important for its health and longevity. This activity has you and your partner connect with couples in different relationship stages so that you can all support one another's relationship journey, sharing your experience and, hopefully, a fun time together.

1. Invite two couples to meet you and your partner for dinner. Select one couple that has been together for less time than you and your partner have and one couple that has been together longer. Explain that you are creating a quarterly couple gathering to strengthen your circle of coupled friends. Be explicit that the goal is friendship connection and shared support of "coupledom."

2. Ask the newest couple to share date ideas. Ask the longest-standing couple to share tips on romance and staying connected. Share tips on planning fun vacations.

3. Let the conversation flow freely, or prepare some questions. A good resource can be found at Today .com/life/relationships/questions-for-couples -rcna73752.

People Who Pamper Together

ACTIVITY TIME:

1½ hours

SUPPLIES:

Ingredients for a homemade facial and hand mask

One of the best benefits of practicing self-care is its positive impact on the people in your life. People learn based on what they see around them, so taking care of yourself often means that those around you start to take better care of themselves, too. But it requires conscious planning to promote self-care to your loved ones. This activity has you explicitly inviting your family or friends to join you in your self-care journey so that they can witness your self-care practice and experience it for themselves.

1. Contact your loved ones and tell them about the fun you've had practicing more self-care. Invite them to your home (or go to theirs) and create a home spa party.

2. Do an internet search of natural spa products using ingredients from your kitchen (e.g., EatingWell.com/article/290952/diy-spa -treatments-you-can-make-in-10-minutes) to make a homemade hand and face mask.

3. Go shopping for ingredients.

4. Set up the products, and have fun making the recipes together.

5. Apply a facial mask and a hand mask for one another.

6. While the masks are on your face, share a story about fun experiences you've had pampering yourself.

7. Follow up the next day to talk about the experience.

Family Connection

ACTIVITY TIME:
30 minutes

SUPPLIES:
Phone

Maintaining close ties with family members and/or childhood friends can be wonderful support for your mental health and well-being. The shared context, history, and cultural connection can help you feel centered and grounded. Many people find as they age, they lose connection with family members and old friends even though they miss them. Of course, you might not desire close relationships with every member, but it is likely there is someone in your family (or chosen family) with whom you would like to deepen the relationship. Those relationships are beneficial, especially in adulthood, because reminiscing about old times can help bring up positive memories of experiences that helped define and shape who you are now.

1. Think about a family member or childhood friend with whom you have positive memories and would like to reconnect. If you are unsure or feel any discomfort reconnecting with someone who comes to mind, hold off on reconnecting for now. Instead, focus on selecting someone with whom the thought of reconnecting lights you up.

2. Get their contact information and call them. When you reach them, say something like "I thought of you the other day and realized how long it's been since we were in touch. I remembered the time that we ..." and launch into reminiscing about a positive connective experience.

3. Continue the conversation, and before ending, agree to chat again in a month.

4. Make sure to reach out again in a month.

Loosen Your Connections

Humans need different types of connections in their lives. It is helpful to have close relationships, yet people should not underestimate the power of loose connections. A loose connection can be the cashier at your local grocery store, the people you see on your regular walk, or the barista at your favorite coffee shop. Interacting with these people can boost happiness and lift your mood. In this activity you'll create a set of loose connections by becoming a regular at a coffee shop in a nearby town. Going to a different town means you'll get out of your routine and increase the likelihood of meeting different people.

1. Do an internet search on "Best coffee shop near me" and pick a four- or five-star establishment that has descriptions like "great service," "nice atmosphere," and, of course, "great coffee or tea." Plan to visit during off-peak hours so there's time to interact and have a seat.

2. During your first visit, make an impression. Ask the cashier how their day is going or, once you taste your beverage, compliment the barista.

3. Plan to stay at least fifteen minutes to savor your beverage slowly. If you feel comfortable, smile at people and say hello.

4. If you see the same barista the next time you go, tell them how much you appreciated the coffee the last time and had to return.

5. Make visits part of your regular weekly routine, and slowly expand your small talk to other regulars you encounter during your visit.

Friend Groups Unite

ACTIVITY TIME:
2 hours

SUPPLIES:
Paper

Pen

A potential reason why it's hard to make time for friendship is that you have multiple friend groups or friend connections that don't overlap. You might focus on a particular set of shared interests with some friends. With other friends, you might focus on something entirely different. That means scheduling separate gatherings with different friends. To combat this, strategically combine your friend groups so that you integrate your life more seamlessly and enrich your experiences by broadening the pool of people that you interact with at one time.

1. Invite your favorite friends or acquaintances to visit your home or another central location for a social gathering. Order takeout or make it a potluck so you can focus on entertaining.

2. Brainstorm a list of the personality traits and interests of all the friends that you will see. Arrange the list into groupings based on any commonalities or themes you see in the list.

3. At the event, introduce each person who comes in and how you know them. Throughout the event, play friend matchmaker by sharing the commonalities you identified between those assembled. For instance, you might say, "Sam, this is Monique; you both love tennis and listening to Afrobeats."

4. Allow the event to flow naturally.

5. Shortly after, ask your friend groups if they would like to set up a group chat to remain connected and schedule future gatherings.

Reunited and Reconnected

ACTIVITY TIME:
20 minutes

SUPPLIES:
None

Friendships are essential. They can be as important as romantic partnerships, and they can support other relationships in your life. Sometimes friends can grow distant from each other because they move into different life stages. Often a conversation about navigating these differences would help, but it rarely happens. Perhaps you have a partner, and your friend does not, or maybe your friend has children, and you don't. Sometimes it's because your career trajectory and theirs take different paths. Recognize that sameness is not required; connection is. Before trying this activity, reflect on whether there are good friends you have distanced yourself from but with whom there is still enough foundation to remain connected.

1. Think about a friend who you would like to feel more connected to and with whom you had a closer friendship in the past.

2. Contact them and arrange a time to chat. Be up front that you value the friendship and hope to talk about maintaining your relationship even when in different life phases. Ask if they would like to have a discussion.

3. When you speak, tell them how much you appreciate and admire them. Acknowledge that things in your lives have changed, and that you realize you have been holding back from sharing your new context.

4. Express your desire to maintain the connection, and explore how your relationship can change to accommodate your current life phases.

Decompression Chamber

ACTIVITY TIME:
1 hour

SUPPLIES:
None

If you live with other people, you spend lots of time together. You get to know one another's ups, downs, and quirks. Although for the most part you might give one another a pass for minor annoyances, you might sometimes repress things or hold grudges that build up over time. It is helpful to develop a habit of discussing communal living concerns. You will likely find that it makes it easier to navigate life challenges or sticky situations together when inevitable difficulties arise.

1. Schedule a regular decompression night, and agree with your cohabitators how often you will hold these sessions.

2. Develop ground rules, such as speaking honestly and directly, using I statements (i.e., "I was happy when . . ." or "I was sad when . . ."), encouraging humor, and trying not to take things personally.

3. During the session, go around to each person and share perspectives on the following:

   a) One thing that is going well

   b) One thing that could be better

   c) One think I'd like to contribute

   d) One request of the other party (or parties)

4. After each person shares, others can respond by saying, "Thank you for sharing."

5. Once everyone has spoken, agree on the most pressing issue to address immediately, and problem-solve together. Make sure to prioritize a different person's needs next session.

Heart Sync

ACTIVITY TIME:
2 minutes

SUPPLIES:
None

Earlier in this book, I shared that hugs were important, even if you are hugging yourself (Give Yourself a Hug, page 22). Research reveals that hugs and touch can promote good sleep, reduce stress, strengthen bonds, and help fight infection by lowering stress hormones. For those reasons, hugs are an important element of social self-care. In this activity, you'll develop a regular hugging and gratitude practice to get the full benefit of touch. By pairing your hug with gratitude for your partner (romantic partner, friend, roommate, etc.), you also practice a key component of well-being. Gratitude has been found to relieve stress, help people bond with others, and reduce anxiety.

1. Stand face-to-face with your partner.

2. Look into your partner's eyes for about thirty seconds while thinking positively about them.

3. Now hug so that you are heart-to-heart with your arms around each other's torso. Hold the hug for forty-five seconds.

4. Now share something you appreciate about your partner, and say "thank you" after they have shared their appreciation.

5. Practice this often to maintain connection.

Hobby Club

ACTIVITY TIME:
Variable

SUPPLIES:
Hobby supplies

So much of adulthood is about moving from task to task; many of you were likely taught from a young age that joy and pleasure were indulgences that wasted your time. Although I hope that the activities in this book help you slow down and practice more self-care and increased connection, I have included this activity as a reminder that it is important to have regular experiences that are not in the pursuit of anything other than joy, to tickle your fancy, light up your life, and experience the freedom of being in the moment. Practice this activity simply because it feels good and gets you immersed. That's right, you deserve a life filled with experiences that bring you pleasure, just for pleasure's sake.

1. Think of a hobby (e.g., ballroom dancing, rock climbing, painting, archery, surfing, hiking, guitar playing) that you have always wanted to try and is accessible in your climate, budget, and comfort level.

2. Do *not* research the pros and cons of the hobby or do an internet search to get proof from others that it is worthwhile. Instead, let your instincts and desire for the hobby be your motivation.

3. Commit to practicing the hobby for at least two months, and find a club or group to do it with.

4. Make room in your calendar to regularly practice your hobby. Take the opportunity to socialize with people in the group or club.

5. Enjoy yourself, and allow yourself to get lost in the activity.

Reclaim Your Culture

ACTIVITY TIME:
30 minutes

SUPPLIES:
Notebook

Pen

Device with internet access

For many people around the world, connection to cultural traditions enhances quality of life. Many facets of culture, such as ethnicity, religion, language, and dialect, contribute to who you are. There can be pressure to conform to the dominant culture and values of the places you live. In this activity, you will reclaim a cultural practice you learned growing up or that you just researched. Connecting to a rich history is a component of social self-care because it lets you deepen your sense of meaning and self-awareness while also letting you feel part of something bigger than yourself. Reminiscing about positive cultural experiences, like the music your family listened to, helps remind you that you are not alone.

1. Write a list of customs you practiced growing up. These are sometimes so ingrained that you don't consider them cultural. Consider practices like home remedies used when sick, how you observed holidays, or the music played in your home.

2. Pick a custom that you recall being soothing or grounding but don't currently practice, and bring it into your current life. For example, if your parents listened to soul music while cleaning the house on Saturday mornings, play that music now, and connect to what it feels like to be part of your people.

3. If you don't recall a custom, do an internet search on local or regional customs from your birthplace or the birthplace of your parents or ancestors. Try a few to determine which is most soothing, and practice it often.

Let's Get Physical

ACTIVITY TIME:

20 minutes

SUPPLIES:

Device with internet access

Phone

Video call platform (most have a free version)

The data show that regular physical activity is one of the best ways to support your mood, body, and overall physical health. Human beings were made to move, yet modern technology and the many comforts of home can make it easy to de-prioritize physical activity. Another challenge to practicing physical activity is that many people learned to focus on exercise for weight loss rather than on all the fun and positive feelings it can bring; this focus leads many people to avoid physical activity altogether. Try physical activity with a social element built in, such as a workout class, a personal trainer, or a group sport. Support your social self-care while you simultaneously benefit your physical, mental, and emotional health.

1. Find an activity buddy willing to schedule a daily (or at least five days a week) twenty-minute movement session with you. Pick someone who also wants more activity. It can be an acquaintance, family member, or good friend. Explain that there is a strong research basis for exercising at least twenty minutes daily.

2. Agree on a time to exercise together, and set up a reoccurring meeting on your free video app.

3. Search for and select five exercise videos that fit your schedule.

4. On the first day, play a video, and exercise with your camera and volume on.

5. Feel free to chat while doing so, and have fun.

Party Like It's 1999!

ACTIVITY TIME:
1 hour

SUPPLIES:
Device to play music

Speakers

Device with internet
   access

Outfits inspired by the
   music (optional)

Trophy (optional)

Listening to music can lower blood pressure and heart rate, lift your mood, and reduce anxiety. You already know about the numerous benefits of physical activity (Let's Get Physical, page 87). So, imagine the power of combining movement and music as a form of social self-care. Music shifts, evolves, and reincarnates, so it can be exciting to expose family members to music from your generation and hear music from theirs. This is a fun activity to do with your children or other young people in your family or circle. I recommend making it a family tradition that you repeat yearly, perhaps during holidays or family gatherings.

1. Invite your family and friends to an era-themed dance party at your home.

2. Ask them to wear outfits inspired by the generation chosen (e.g., '50s, '80s, '00s) with clothes they have on hand. Send photos of that time for inspiration.

3. Gather your family and friends for the party, and play music from that era.

4. Beforehand, research popular dances from the time, and teach them during the party.

5. If your family enjoys a bit of healthy competition, purchase a trophy to give to the best dancer.

6. Next time, pick a new family member to lead, and pass the trophy to the next winner.

7. Congratulations, you have a new tradition.

Musical Drive of Wonder

ACTIVITY TIME:

3 hours

SUPPLIES:

Device to play music

Car

Journal

Pen

When you connect with another person and enjoy their company, you are creating a flood of positive emotions in your body. In turn, your positive emotions feed and amplify the positive emotions of the person you're with. Memories of positive moments can help you widen your perspective and gain a fuller picture. This activity blends the curative power of music, positive connection, and shared novel experiences. You can do it with a partner, child, sibling, parent, or friend.

1. Create a playlist of songs from key positive moments in your life, such as a graduation, prom, or milestone birthday,

2. Go for a drive with the person you've picked for this activity, and head to a new destination for both of you.

3. Play songs from your playlist on your way there. Share the context for each song and, in doing so, share a bit of your life.

4. When you arrive at your destination, explore it together. On the way back, listen to songs from the other person's playlist, enjoy them, and give your full attention to their stories about the connection between them and the music.

5. Write the playlist and key memories of the day in a journal where you recount your favorite memories.

CHAPTER 5

Professional Self-Care

Your Productive Three

ACTIVITY TIME:

3 hours

SUPPLIES:

Planner or calendar

Pen

When our to-dos feel unending, it can lead to a lacking sense of accomplishment. But learning to prioritize tasks by identifying the three most important for the day will give you an objective measurement. For this activity, focus on selecting three tasks per day. Because research indicates that most people are productive for about three hours a day, you will identify tasks you can complete or on which you can make significant progress in about three hours.

1. At the start of your workweek, write out a list of tasks you plan to accomplish, being mindful that other responsibilities requiring your attention might pop up throughout the week.

2. Assuming you work a five-day week, review your list, and pick the fifteen most important tasks to accomplish for the week. Note that some of your tasks might be interrelated and require you to complete one first before moving to the next, so factor that in.

3. On day one, pick three tasks to work on—one challenging and two important, but with lower stakes—and write them in your calendar for the day. Plan to do the work within three hours. Note: If unanticipated tasks come up, it's okay to switch out what you intended to complete with a new task or to do it in the remaining time you have in the day.

4. At the end of the day, cross the tasks off your to-do list. Congratulate yourself on the progress you made. Continue the process each day of the week.

Work Bestie Career Coach

ACTIVITY TIME:
30 minutes

SUPPLIES:
Calendar

Having at least one person at work with whom you can have honest and candid conversations can help you release the stressors associated with work. I recommend that my clients schedule a weekly conversation with a work friend to do what authors Amelia Nagoski and Emily Nagoski call "completing the stress cycle." This means that people must find consistent ways to release stress to signal to their bodies that the threat of their daily stressors is over. The most effective way to release the stress is through daily physical activity. Talking with a confidant is the second.

1. Think about a colleague that you'd like to connect with on a weekly basis. If you have a colleague you trust and whose company you enjoy, contact them to schedule. If you still need a work bestie, consider who you'd like to get to know better. You might need a series of coffee or walk dates with a few different people until you find your person.

2. When you've found your work bestie, agree on a regular meeting time, plan for at least thirty minutes, and make a reoccurring appointment to go for a walk or do another activity that is easy to do during the workday.

3. Split the time equally to discuss how your work life is going. Share positive happenings, discuss career concerns, and ask for advice about work situations. Sometimes you might need to vent or gain perspective.

4. When the relationship is new, introduce more minor issues and over time more complex ones.

Grow Your Mindset

ACTIVITY TIME:

30 minutes

SUPPLIES:

Journal

Pen

Psychologist Carol Dweck coined the term *growth mindset* to describe the fact that humans have the capacity to grow and that their strengths are not set in stone. A growth mindset can help build resilience and self-esteem. I find that teaching the concept of a growth mindset to clients going through career transitions helps them understand that even though they might need to develop new skills for the next phase of their work life (including preparing for retirement), they are capable of doing so.

1. When preparing for your next career phase requires knowledge, experience, or skill, notice your emotional reaction and thoughts about your perceived gap between knowledge and experience. Tell yourself, "I bet there is an opportunity for growth during this challenge; let me explore."

2. Journal about your thoughts related to this experience to excavate and release your concerns.

3. Write a list of other situations over the course of your life that required you to gain experience, go through trial and error, or even fail before you experienced success.

4. Reverse engineer your successes to determine the strategies you used to meet your goals, and apply them to the current situation.

Daily Transition Ritual

ACTIVITY TIME:

15 minutes

SUPPLIES:

Lavender or chamomile
 tea

Pen

Journal

As one component of professional self-care, it is helpful to have a ritual that signals you are boundary crossing, or transitioning from your work self to your home self. This helps you switch off your work brain and allows you to be present for who you are beyond your job. Boundary crossing can be changing out of your work clothes to home clothes, sipping a beverage when you arrive home, or even taking several deep breaths before opening the door to your residence. For this activity, I will guide you through boundary crossing, and you can replace the activity I have offered with one that feels more relevant. I recommend creating a habit of engaging in a boundary crossing activity each day that you work in or outside the home.

1. When you arrive home from work or finish working for the day, make a cup of herbal tea; consider chamomile or lavender (check with your doctor for any contraindications) as both have been found to relieve stress and anxiety. Sit down in a comfortable chair.

2. While the tea cools, do a mind dump by jotting down any work-related thoughts you are carrying from the day. As you close the journal, imagine putting the thoughts away in a box on a shelf until the next day.

3. Drink your tea slowly, breathing softly between sips until you finish.

4. Notice the sense of calm and tension relief as you congratulate yourself for taking the time.

5. Continue with the rest of your routine for the day.

Body First

ACTIVITY TIME:
5 minutes

SUPPLIES:
None

No matter what stage of your professional life you are in, you likely have to deal with multiple deadlines or handle challenging colleagues, for instance, which requires coping skills. These experiences might trigger a stress reaction that leads to a range of responses known as fight, flight, freeze, or fawn. When in these states, your survival brain kicks in, and it can be challenging to use the problem-solving areas of your brain effectively. To free you to think through next steps, first, try tending to your bodily reaction to the stressor.

1. Think of a work situation that is mildly challenging and that you cope with regularly.

2. Make a mental note that the next time you experience this situation, you will do a breathing exercise before taking any other action.

3. The next time you experience the situation when working, pause and notice your breath.

4. Slow your breath by breathing in through your nose for a count of four, pausing for a count of four, and breathing out from your mouth for a count of four.

5. Pause for a count of four, and repeat for at least five breaths.

6. Scan your body for signs of discomfort, and continue breathing in this manner as until you calm your body.

7. Once you have mastered this practice for mildly challenging situations, apply it to more challenging ones.

Daydream Your Way to Your Career Move

ACTIVITY TIME:
30 minutes

SUPPLIES:
Paper

Pen

Device with internet access

You can harness the power of visualization to see the future outcome you desire. When you visualize, you shift your sense of self to that of a person who has met the goal, and you build your confidence in achieving it. Doing this primes your brain to take the opportunities in your life to bring you closer to the hoped-for outcome. For this activity, you'll start by identifying a professional goal and spend time imagining yourself reaching it.

1. Think about the next big step you want to take in your career. Write about what you'll experience when you have reached that goal by using your senses (e.g., sight, smell, hearing, taste, and touch) to describe what your life will be like. For example, "I walk into the building where my new job is, and the lobby is bright and sun filled, and I am full of excitement" or "When I tell my best friend that I got the job, they give me the best hug ever as we scream with joy."

2. Spend five minutes a day for a week visualizing your life after having met your goal.

3. Over the next week, take actions inspired by your goal, like connecting with people on LinkedIn who work at a company of interest, or telling friends and acquaintances that you are looking for a new opportunity. Also, consider preparing your résumé and applying for jobs.

4. Commit to taking opportunities that present themselves and that align with your goals.

Prep Your Response

ACTIVITY TIME:
10 minutes

SUPPLIES:
Paper
Pen

A microaggression is an indirect, subtle, or unintentional discrimination against members of a marginalized group. For women in the workplace, microaggressions come in many shapes and sizes: questioning competence, asking you to tone it down, company policies that prohibit natural hairstyles, or people taking credit for your work or calling you a "girl." Microaggressions often take you by surprise and bring about an emotional reaction, making it challenging to think about a response in the moment. Experiencing microaggressions can contribute to racial trauma, increase anxiety and cortisol, and lower confidence and work satisfaction. You can prepare for some of the common microaggressions that you face by planning your responses in advance. Unfortunately, in work environments, microaggressions can reoccur because you are exposed to the same people, so you will likely have an opportunity to use your response more than once.

1. Think about microaggressions you experience in your professional life, ones where you wish you had an appropriate verbal response.

2. On a piece of paper, create two columns: On the left column, title it "Microaggression," and on the right column, "My response."

3. List each possible microaggression and a response you can use the next time someone commits that microaggression against you.

4. Here are some sample response statements:

   a) No, you cannot touch my hair.

   b) I am uncomfortable with the implications of your statement.

   c) Can you explain what you mean? I am not sure I understand.

   d) I prefer to be addressed by my name, not as one of "the girls."

5. Practice making these statements in advance until you can state them with confidence.

Your Power Source

ACTIVITY TIME:
2 minutes

SUPPLIES:
Photos or items in your home

Calendar with reminders setting

You probably can tell that I think women are amazing. We have the potential to be and do anything that we set our minds to. Admittedly, daily life responsibilities and tasks can disconnect you from awareness of your innate strength, talent, and power. Because of this, it is helpful to have visual reminders of just how powerful and strong you are. And don't forget that there is power and strength in admitting when you're tired or vulnerable, crying or laughing when you need to, and even sometimes shouting. In this activity, you'll gather two or three items from your home to put in your workspace that remind you of your power.

1. Walk around your home and visually scan for items that you enjoy looking at that engender a sense of power and mastery. This can be a framed quote or affirmation, a photo of yourself or your family, an award, or a portrait of a nature scene that evokes these feelings.

2. Touch the contenders and notice how you feel doing so. Pick two or three that bring about the most positive feelings, and take them to your workspace. If you don't have a dedicated workspace, you can take a photo.

3. Place two reminders in your calendar to glance at your items (or photos) during your day. As you do, take note of the positive physical (e.g., warm fuzzy feeling) and emotional (e.g., pride) signals you have, and allow yourself to enjoy them for a moment or two before returning to your task.

Multitask No More

ACTIVITY TIME:
Variable

SUPPLIES:
None

In Conscious Uncoupling (page 57), you experienced how multitasking can affect your personal life. Now you'll see the repercussions it has for your professional life. Multitasking involves working on more than one task at a time, like checking your email when in a meeting. When you switch between tasks, it takes time to refocus on the original task. Multitasking can also lead to errors and makes it more challenging to sustain your attention over time. Multitasking can lead to a false sense of getting more done and saving time. Instead, multitasking has been found to contribute to lower productivity and increased stress. This activity will help you counteract multitasking by limiting distractions (e.g., surfing the internet when in a meeting) and segmenting your work into manageable parts. You can pair this activity with Your Productive Three (page 92) at the top of the chapter.

1. Consider the most common distractions that you face during your workday. Typical examples include scrolling on your phone, searching the internet, checking email, and conversing with others.

2. Before you begin one of your key tasks for the day, clear your workspace and computer (if you use one) of distractions. For example, put your phone out of sight, put on headphones if you work in a group setting, turn off your internet if you don't need it for the task, and if colleagues can see your calendar, place a note that states you are busy and give a time when you will respond to messages. If

continued ➔

there is an expectation that you respond to messages quickly, inform people in advance that you will do so at specific times of the day.

3. Determine how much time (e.g., twenty-five-minute work blocks as described in the Pomodoro Technique; see the Resources section, page 117) you will allot to your first task, and focus on it interruption-free for the duration.

4. If you feel tempted by distraction, pause, take a deep breath, and remind yourself, "I am focusing for just a bit longer."

5. When you are done, pause before moving to your next task.

Pleasure and Joy Breaks

ACTIVITY TIME:
15 minutes

SUPPLIES:
Paper
Pen
Timer

Pleasure is an important factor in living a fulfilled and joyful life. Some women fear that if they open themselves to a bit of pleasure, they won't be able to focus on life responsibilities. But taking a break for pleasure actually makes you more productive; studies reveal that pleasure breaks can lower anxiety and stress so that you can concentrate better afterward. Plus, I believe that pleasure has a place in every aspect of life—even work. This activity will help you create breaks throughout the workday to bring more pleasure into your professional life—what better way to be more productive, prevent burnout, and otherwise care for yourself professionally?

1. Write a list of activities that bring you pleasure that you can do in short bursts during your day and fit into your work context. Examples include coloring, reading, daydreaming, listening to music, dancing, and meditating.

2. Pick five activities from your list, and plan to build them into your schedule for the upcoming week.

3. Schedule at least one fifteen-minute break per day to engage in your pleasurable activity, and set an alarm when it is time to begin.

4. At the appointed time, have fun doing your activity, making sure to set a timer for when your fifteen minutes are up.

5. Before going back to work, congratulate yourself for taking a pleasure break!

Get Outside and Recharge Your Battery

ACTIVITY TIME:
20 minutes

SUPPLIES:
Calendar with
reminders

Timer

Getting regular fresh air and sun holds many benefits and should not be relegated just to after work or weekends. Research has found that going outside during your workday is a restorative experience with cognitive and physical benefits. Getting at least twenty minutes of sun daily can provide a natural mood boost from the vitamin D. And, as you know from Pleasure and Joy Breaks (page 103), a brief break can bring more productivity. When you expend so much energy working, it is okay and necessary to take moments of rest. Combining a rest with time in the sun and fresh air is a priceless way to care for yourself during the workday.

1. Set a reoccurring appointment in your calendar for a twenty-minute recharge session each day you work. Make a mental commitment to keep this appointment with yourself and to reschedule it for the same day if your schedule changes.

2. Think about where you can be outside comfortably with some aspect of nature (e.g., grass, trees, birds) and plan a backup option in case it's unavailable.

3. When the time comes, go outside for twenty minutes; set your phone timer. If you are comfortable doing so, don't bring something for entertainment. Just rest and take in the sights and sounds around you.

4. Focus your attention on the natural landscape, the blades of grass, trees, the skyline, or sounds of the birds—or just be.

Email Clearing

ACTIVITY TIME:

2 hours

SUPPLIES:

Email access

Cheryl Richardson's classic book *The Art of Extreme Self-Care* highlights the emotional load of seemingly small things that can affect your well-being. For many people, email can be one of those hidden stressors. There is probably an ever-growing queue of emails flooding your inboxes daily, and those that require an immediate response most often capture your attention and time. There are, however, several emails you read that, for a myriad of reasons, you do not want to respond to now— some because they do not require a right-now response and others because you want to think about the appropriate response to make. These "put-off" emails risk being forgotten in the shuffle of life. Scheduling some time every week to catch up on these delayed-response messages can be a massive stress release. Consider the Organize Your Inbox activity (page 70) to declutter personal emails.

1. Clear an afternoon at the end of the week, grab something you enjoy drinking, and sit in a comfortable chair from which you can work on your computer.

2. Go back to all those emails you've opened in the past week but have yet to respond to, and begin your review.

3. For those that warrant a response, take on the ones that require the least thought and shortest answers first to get momentum going and to allow yourself to feel a sense of accomplishment.

continued →

4. Move to the emails that require a more thoughtful response. Take your time with them, think them through, and draft appropriate and considered responses.

5. When you are done, relish the relief and calm you feel after releasing those emails from your to do list.

6. Consider giving yourself a reward for a job well done.

Lunch Break Your Way

ACTIVITY TIME:
30 minutes

SUPPLIES:
Lunch ingredients
Timer or alarm
Reading materials

Since the pandemic, working from home has continued to be a popular arrangement for numerous workers. Although people have come to grips with the advantages and challenges of doing so, one of the practices that many are still wrestling with is taking an actual lunch break. In the office, lunch was likely an opportunity to engage in fellowship with your peers or a time to allow yourself a period of idle relaxation; at home, however, eating times can be sporadic, and many people even multitask while continuing to work. Taking lunch breaks away from work tasks is important for sustenance, digestion, satisfaction, refueling, and concentration.

1. At the beginning of every week, plan your lunches, and obtain any groceries you need for your meals.

2. Set a notification on your computer or phone to remind you of your lunch break.

3. Move away from your workstation to a more relaxed location in your home where you can eat your food without digital or technological distractions. Set out your lunch on a plate, and use real utensils.

4. Collect a group of reading materials—either newspapers, magazines, or books—and relax and read them after eating. Spend at least twenty minutes at lunch.

5. Pay attention to your notification telling you your lunch break is over. Clear your dishes, return to work, and notice the increased calm from taking a break.

Reclaiming My Time

ACTIVITY TIME:
1 minute

SUPPLIES:
Phone

Phones can be a helpful tool to connect with people whenever you need to. Complete accessibility without a break, however, can drive you to distraction and, paradoxically, disconnection. In times past, people would leave their offices at 5:00 p.m. without further access to computers or work landline phones, and they were free to live as they saw fit until the next day. But with email and messaging on everyone's smartphones, it can be easy to stay connected to the office long after you have physically left, or stopped working for the day. And this relentless contact with work can negatively impact personal relationships, decrease motivation, and contribute to burnout. It is time to take back your life and disconnect from work (as much as is possible in your context), and this activity can help you do just that.

1. Think about how you want to separate your work and personal communication. You might consider having two cell phones (one for work and one for your personal life), keeping all your work-related communication on your work laptop, or using apps on your phone for work that you can easily turn off at the end of the day.

2. Determine what your workday hours should optimally be.

3. Put your working hours in your public work calendar or otherwise notify your colleagues of the hours you are available.

4. At the end of your workday, turn off the ringer on your work phone and place it in a desk drawer, or, turn off your work laptop and put it away. If you have apps you use for work on your personal phone, silence them. Resist the temptation to check in on work before you begin your workday the next day.

5. If you feel uncomfortable about not checking in, it is helpful to remember that the discomfort is likely your brain looking for you to engage in your regular habit, not that there is a problem.

Morning Routine

ACTIVITY TIME:
15 to 30 minutes

SUPPLIES:
Varied

When you create a morning routine, you consciously set the tone for the rest of your day so that you begin work feeling calmer, can think more clearly, and are nimbler in dealing with the challenges of the day. In effect, you're telling your nervous system it is safe to go about the rest of your day. If you begin your day by checking your phone or email, caretaking, or rushing through your hygiene and nutritional needs and then getting right to work, it can negatively influence your mood and sense of purpose. Some women need the same morning routine every day; others might benefit from having a variety of activities that they can choose from. You decide what works best for you.

1. Pick one or two activities (e.g., journaling, crocheting, yoga, writing poetry) you enjoy and can complete within fifteen to thirty minutes during your morning routine.

2. Set up any supplies that you need the night before.

3. Go to bed each night of your workweek in enough time to get the number of hours you require and to wake up fifteen to thirty minutes earlier.

4. If you live with other people, let them know you're unavailable during this time, or wake up before they do to limit interruptions.

5. Upon waking, take a few moments to center yourself and do your morning activity.

Creating Options

ACTIVITY TIME:
2 hours

SUPPLIES:
Computer
Résumé

The best way to develop professionally is to be imagining advancement opportunities. It's in your best interest to always be looking for a new job, not just being open to hearing about new opportunities but actively creating and pursuing them. The first time you practice this activity, you'll need about two hours. After that, accomplish what you can in an hour, and you'll likely find that it gets easier and takes less time as you get into a routine.

1. Every quarter, schedule a career date with yourself. Update your résumé, adding in new skills and new responsibilities you have undertaken.

2. Keep in contact with one or two recruiters who specialize in your profession, sending them updated résumés and discussing with them the types of opportunities they are seeing.

3. Stay abreast of the online job boards that post about your profession, and determine the types of jobs that would be an advance over what you are currently doing.

4. Apply to jobs that pique your interest; do not worry if you don't meet all the criteria. Research demonstrates that women are more likely to count themselves in only if they meet 100 percent of the criteria, whereas men apply when they only meet some of the requirements.

5. Take interviews for jobs that seem interesting.

Visualize Your Impact

ACTIVITY TIME:
1 hour

SUPPLIES:
Graph paper
Writing instruments

Work often plays a vital role in your sense of meaning. Whatever your position is, it allows you to develop new skills, help others, create solutions for problems, or serve a mission. Try keeping track of the impact of your work, and review it often to help you remember and celebrate your contributions. Doing so supports your career self-efficacy, which is the belief that your actions can bring about your desired career outcomes. This activity will guide you to trace your job roles, responsibilities, and accomplishments and create a time line of them. You will track your career growth and gauge your progress. This vantage point can help raise your self-esteem and give you a clearer sense of the difference you are making.

1. Get some graph paper and a variety of colored pencils/pens.

2. Draw a horizontal line across the center of the page and evenly space out the names of all the adult jobs you've held from left to right.

3. Below each job, write or draw highlights of your experience in the role.

4. On the vertical axis, starting where the lines meet, write "0" and evenly space the numbers vertically until you reach 10.

5. Rate your level of impact at each job from 0 (low) to 10 (high), and connect the dots.

6. Take several minutes to review your creation and take in the progress of your impact.

7. Share it with a supportive person in your life who can reflect your brilliance back to you.

See It and Believe It

ACTIVITY TIME:
1 hour

SUPPLIES:
Paper

Pen

Device with internet access

As an undergraduate student, when I saw another Black woman close in age studying to get her doctorate in counseling psychology, I knew that I could achieve my own dream. Right now, you may have dreams of launching your own business, moving into a new career, or ascending the ranks at your current employer, but you need to figure out how. This activity encourages you to consider women who have already done what you seek to.

1. Write down your ideal career path. Look for biographical material about those whose career path models yours and determine the work tools they used to get there.

2. Being brutally honest, write down the tools you will need to acquire to achieve your goal successfully.

3. Determine who would be the best teacher or guide for each of the tools you need.

4. Determine how those tools can be obtained: college courses, professional workshops sponsored by your field's professional/union organization, work-related conferences, internships, one-on-one mentorships, etc.

5. Invest the time and resources to start acquiring whatever you need to become who you want to be.

Vacation Scheduling

ACTIVITY TIME:
45 minutes

SUPPLIES:
Calendar

Each year, American workers leave a surprising amount of annual vacation time left on the table. Does this sound like you? How much annual leave do you carry over from year to year? Some think it is a badge of honor not to take vacations, feeling like they are indispensable or that it's too much of a hassle because work will pile up when they are gone. The fact of the matter is that taking your vacation time is critically necessary for your optimal functioning, well-being, and growth and development. Not every vacation requires planning a big trip. Sometimes it merely entails taking a day or two strategically to recharge and take care of your mind, body, and soul.

1. At the beginning of each year, divide your vacation time into three parts: the "Long Break," the "Short Break," and the "Self-Care Break."

2. With the Long Break, devote at least half of your vacation time to taking an away-from-home vacation if that is feasible for you.

3. With the Short Break, chart out some three- or four-day weekends where you can rest either at home or close by at a bed-and-breakfast or an Airbnb.

4. With the Self-Care Break, save them for days when you need to take unplanned time to tend to your mental health and energy.

5. Turn in your vacation requests first thing in January to lock in your days.

Creative Spark

ACTIVITY TIME:
5 minutes

SUPPLIES:

Pen or pencil

Sticky note

Notepad and paper or recording device

Creativity can manifest in the way you develop ideas. When you are working on a new idea but cannot get started, you might think you are procrastinating. Although sometimes that is the case, it's important to dig a little deeper. Sometimes the delay might be that you are working on a problem in your mind before it translates into a clear message. This activity encourages you not to judge yourself, but to capture inspiration when it strikes.

1. Think of a work project or task you are having trouble initiating, and write a brief description of it on a sticky note. Write (or draw) the outcome you are planning. Place the note somewhere you will see it at least once a day so that you can keep it top of mind.

2. Use a notepad or recording device to write down any ideas that come up during your day.

3. When you start to feel clear about the direction, schedule a work session, and let your ideas and the project flow.

4. If you still have difficulty, it might be because your stress level is too high. Take a break using one of the break activities in this chapter to clear your mind and lower stress to a level that allows you to work rather than feel stuck.

5. Before you know it, you'll have gotten your project underway and started to make progress.

Resources

CicelyBrathwaite.com

My website features information about how to improve your self-care and well-being at work and in your daily life. Visit the book and resource pages.

HeartMath Institute
heartmath.org

Heartmath is an organization dedicated to helping people better handle stress and build resilience.

Homecoming: Overcome Fear and Trauma to Reclaim Your Whole, Authentic Self by Thema Bryant-Davis, PhD

This book helps the reader deepen self-awareness and feel empowered to heal and build resilience.

My Grandmother's Hands: Racialized Trauma and the Pathway to Mending Our Hearts and Bodies by Resmaa Menakem, MSW, LICSW, SEP

This powerful book helps readers incorporate strategies that support their physical, mental, and emotional well-being.

Own Your Greatness: Overcome Impostor Syndrome, Beat Self-Doubt, and Succeed in Life by Lisa Orbé-Austin, PhD, and Richard Orbé-Austin, PhD

This book helps readers understand that imposter syndrome is not inevitable and can be resolved using emotional and mental strategies.

Pomodoro Technique

**todoist.com/productivity-methods
/pomodoro-technique**

The Pomodoro Technique is a great way to stay on top of your tasks and also give yourself the time to rest and refocus.

Tapping Solution

thetappingsolution.com/#home-optin

This app is full of emotional freedom technique (EFT) tapping meditations. EFT is an emerging evidence-based practice for lowering stress chemicals associated with a variety of life stressors.

We Should All Be Millionaires: A Woman's Guide to Earning More, Building Wealth, and Gaining Economic Power by Rachel Rodgers

This book sheds insight into how readers can support their professional, mental, and emotional self-care through economic empowerment.

References

Comer, Jeff. "The Fallacy of Multitasking." *Psychology Today*, March 17, 2022. Accessed April 13, 2023. psychologytoday.com/us/blog/beyond-stress-and-burnout/202203/the-fallacy-multitasking#:~:text=The%20human%20brain%20cannot%20multitask,stress%2C%20and%20leads%20to%20burnout.

Dalton-Smith, Saundra. *Sacred Rest: Recover Your Life, Renew Your Energy, Restore Your Sanity.* New York: FaithWords, 2019.

Dweck, Carol S. *Mindset: The New Psychology of Success.* New York: Random House, 2016.

Gonzalo, Angelo, "Dorothea Orem: Self-Care Deficit Theory." *Nurseslabs,* updated January 12, 2023. Accessed April 25, 2023. nurseslabs.com/dorothea-orems-self-care-theory.

McGlone, Francis, and Susannah Walker. "Four Ways Hugs Are Good for Your Health." *Greater Good,* June 22, 2021. Accessed April 13, 2023. greatergood.berkeley.edu/article/item/four_ways_hugs_are_good_for_your_health.

Nagoski, Emily, and Amelia Nagoski. *Burnout: The Secret to Unlocking the Stress Cycle.* New York: Ballantine Books, 2020.

Neuroscience News. "Art Evokes Feelings in the Body." *Neuroscience News,* March 27, 2023. Accessed April 23, 2023. neurosciencenews.com/art-body-emotion-22883.

"The Number One Habit to Develop in Order to Feel More Positive." *Amen Clinics,* August 16, 2016. Accessed April 11, 2023. amenclinics.com/blog/number-one-habit-develop-order-feel-positive.

Ornstein, Robert E., and David S. Sobel. *Healthy Pleasures.* Reading, MA: Addison-Wesley, 1989.

Richardson, Cheryl. *The Art of Extreme Self-Care.* Chicago: Hay House, Inc., 2009.

Speaking of Psychology. "Why Clutter Stresses Us Out, with Dn. Joseph Ferrari, Phd." *American Psychological Association.* Accessed April 11, 2023. apa.org/news/podcasts/speaking-of-psychology/clutter.

Stanley, Elizabeth A. *Widen the Window: Training Your Brain and Body to Thrive during Stress and Recover from Trauma.* London: Yellow Kite, 2021.

Thorpe, Matthew. "12 Benefits of Meditation." *Healthline,* October 27, 2020. Accessed April 24, 2023. healthline.com/nutrition/12-benefits-of -meditation.

Wilcox, Gloria. "The Feeling Wheel - The Gottman Institute." The Gottman Institute. Accessed September 18, 2023. https://cdn.gottman.com /wp-content/uploads/2020/12/The-Gottman-Institute_The-Feeling -Wheel_v2.pdf.

Index

Notes